CIVILIZATION AND TRANSCENDENCE

Other BBT Publications

Books by His Divine Grace
A.C. Bhaktivedanta Swami Prabhupada

Bhagavad-gītā As It Is
Śrīmad-Bhāgavatam, Cantos 1-12 (18 vols.)
Śrī Caitanya-caritāmṛta (17 vols.)
Teachings of Lord Caitanya
The Nectar of Devotion
The Nectar of Instruction
Śrī Īśopaniṣad
Easy Journey to Other Planets
Kṛṣṇa Consciousness: The Topmost Yoga System
Kṛṣṇa, the Supreme Personality of Godhead
Perfect Questions, Perfect Answers
Teachings of Lord Kapila
Teachings of Queen Kuntī
The Path of Perfection
Kṛṣṇa, the Reservoir of Pleasure
The Science of Self-Realization
The Journey of Self-Discovery
A Second Chance: The Story of a Near-Death Experience
Preaching Is the Essence
Life Comes From Life
The Perfection of Yoga
Beyond Birth and Death
On the Way to Kṛṣṇa
Rāja-vidyā: The King of Knowledge
Elevation to Kṛṣṇa Consciousness
Kṛṣṇa Consciousness: The Matchless Gift
Message of Godhead
Back to Godhead magazine (founder)

Available from:

The Bhaktivedanta Book Trust
3764 Watseka Ave.
Los Angeles
CA 90034, USA

The Bhaktivedanta Book Trust
P.O. Box 324
Borehamwood, Hers.
WD6 1NB, U.K.

The Bhaktivedanta Book Trust
P.O. Box 262
Botany, N.S.W
2019 Australia

ALL GLORY TO SRI GURU AND GAURANGA

CIVILIZATION AND TRANSCENDENCE

His Divine Grace

A.C. BHAKTIVEDANTA SWAMI PRABHUPADA

Founder-acharya of the International Society for Krishna Consciousness

THE BHAKTIVEDANTA BOOK TRUST

Readers interested in the subject matter of this book are invited to correspond with the Secretary (for a full list in each country please see the back of this book):

International Society for Krishna Consciousness
3764 Watseka Avenue, Los Angeles,
California 90034, USA

International Society for Krishna Consciousness
P.O. Box 324, Borehamwood, Herts.,
WD6 1NB, U.K.

International Society for Krishna Consciousness
P.O. Box 159, Kings Cross,
N.S.W. 2011, Australia

First Printing, 1990: 200,000 copies

Printed in USA

ISBN: 0-89213-298-1

Contents

His Divine Grace A. C. Bhaktivedanta Swami Prabhupāda replies to a Questionnaire from Bhavan's Journal
June 28, 1976

RELIGION WITH NO CONCEPTION OF GOD?

Puṣṭa Kṛṣṇa: Śrīla Prabhupāda, this questionnaire was sent to you by *Bhavan's Journal*, a cultural and religious magazine in Bombay. They are questioning various religious and spiritual leaders, trying to get the answers to some of the important questions that are perplexing people today. So there's a list of questions, and the first is this: "Is the influence of religion over the masses on the wane?"

Śrīla Prabhupāda: Yes. This is predicted in *Śrīmad-Bhāgavatam* [12.2.1]:

tataś cānu-dinaṁ dharmaḥ
satyaṁ śaucaṁ kṣamā dayā
kālena balinā rājan
naṅkṣyaty āyur balaṁ smṛtiḥ

"In Kali-yuga, this age of quarrel and hypocrisy, there shall be a waning of these qualities: religiosity, truthfulness, cleanliness, tolerance, memory, bodily strength, duration of life, and mercy." These are the human assets—qualities which make a human being distinct from the animals. But these things will decline. There will be almost no mercy, there will be almost no truthfulness, memory will be shortened, duration of life shortened. Similarly, religion will practically vanish. So that means gradually human beings will descend to the platform of animals.

Especially when there is no religion, human beings are simply animals. This any common man can distinguish—that a dog does not understand what religion is. The dog is also a living being, but he's not interested in what is being discussed here about *Bhagavad-gītā* or *Śrīmad-Bhāgavatam*. That is the distinction between man and dog: the animal is not interested. So when human beings are becoming uninterested in religion, then they're becoming animals.

And how can there be happiness or peace in animal society? The big leaders want to keep the citizenry as animals, and at the same time they are striving to make a United Nations. How is it possible? United Animals? Is it possible? Society for United Animals. [*Laughter*.] In the science of logic it is said, "Man is a rational animal." So when rationality is missing, one becomes simply an animal. What is the possibility of being a human being?

In human society, whether you are a Christian or a Muhammadan or a Hindu or a Buddhist, it doesn't matter. But there must be some system of religion—that is human society. And human society without religion—animal society. This is the plain fact. Why are people unhappy now? Because they are neglecting religion.

One gentleman has written me that Marx said, "Religion is the opium of the people." That means the Communists are very adamant against God consciousness because they think that religion has spoiled the whole social atmosphere. Religion might have been misused, but that does not mean that religion should be avoided. Real religion should be taken. Simply because religion has not been properly executed by the so-called priests, that does not mean religion should be rejected. If my eye is giving me some kind of trouble on account of a cataract, that doesn't mean my eye should be plucked out. The cataract should be removed. So that is the idea of the Kṛṣṇa consciousness movement—to remove the cataract from people's religious vision.

Generally, modern so-called religious leaders have no conception of God, and yet they are preaching religion. What good is that religion? People are simply being misled. Real religion means God's order: *dharmaṁ tu sākṣād bhagavat-praṇītam*. If your religion has no conception of God, where is the question of religion? Still, without any conception of God, they are professing some religion. How long will it go on artificially? It will deteriorate. That ignorance about God has resulted in the present condition.

Religion means the order of God, just as law means the order of the state. Now, if in your social system there is no state, where is the question of the state's order? You will simply manufacture your own order. Today that is going on in the field of religion: there is no conception of God and therefore no following of God's order.

But we devotees of Kṛṣṇa have a clear conception of God. Here is God: Kṛṣṇa. And He's giving orders. We accept those orders. So it is clear religion. But if there is no conception of God, no order of God, then where is the question of religion? Ask someone in some other religious system what their conception of the form of God is. Can anyone tell clearly? Nobody can say. But we shall immediately say,

veṇuṁ kvaṇantam aravinda-dalāyatākṣaṁ
barhāvataṁsam asitāmbudha-sundarāṅgam
kandarpa-koṭi-kamanīya-viśeṣa-śobhaṁ
govindam ādi-puruṣaṁ tam ahaṁ bhajāmi

"I worship Govinda, the primeval Lord, who is adept at playing on His flute, whose eyes are like petals of a blooming lotus, whose head is bedecked with a peacock's feather, whose figure of beauty is tinged with the hue of blue clouds, and whose unique loveliness charms millions of Cupids." [*Brahma-saṁhitā* 5.30]

Immediately, description—"Here is God." Then there is religion. And if there is no conception of God, where is the question of religion? Bogus. That is why religiosity and the other noble human qualities are declining. People have no conception of God, and therefore there is no understanding of religion. As a result, the whole human civilization is declining. And because it is declining, human beings are becoming more and more like animals.

PROGRESSING BEYOND "PROGRESS"

Puṣṭa Kṛṣṇa: Question number two?
Śrīla Prabhupāda: Yes.
Puṣṭa Kṛṣṇa: "The traditional charge against Hinduism is that it is fatalistic, that it inhibits progress by making

people slaves to the belief in the inevitability of what is to happen. How far is this charge true?"

Śrīla Prabhupāda: The charge is false. Those who have made that charge do not know what "Hinduism" is. First of all, the Vedic scriptures make no mention of such a thing as "Hinduism." but they do mention *sanātana-dharma*, the eternal and universal religion, and also *varṇāśrama-dharma*, the natural organization of human society. That we can find in the Vedic scriptures.

So it is a false charge that the Vedic system inhibits the progress of mankind. What is that "progress"? A dog's jumping is progress? [*Laughter.*] A dog is running here and there on four legs, and you are running on four wheels. Is that progress?

The Vedic system is this: The human being has a certain amount of energy—better energy than the animals', better consciousness—and that energy should be utilized for spiritual advancement. So the whole Vedic system is meant for spiritual advancement. Human energy is employed in a more exalted direction than to compete with the dog.

Consequently, sometimes those who have no idea of religion notice that the Indian saintly persons are not working hard like dogs. Spiritually uncultured people think the dog race is life. But actual life is spiritual progress. Therefore the *Śrīmad-Bhagavatam* [1.5.18] says,

tasyaiva hetoḥ prayateta kovido
na labhyate yad bhramatām upary adhaḥ
tal labhyate duḥkhavad anyataḥ sukhaṁ
kālena sarvatra gabhīra-raṁhasā

The human being should exert his energy for that thing which he did not get in many, many lives. Through many, many lives the soul has been in the forms of dogs or demigods or cats or birds or insects. There are 8,400,000 material forms. So this transmigration is going on, but in every one of these millions of forms, the business is sense gratification. The dog is busy for sense gratification: "Where is food? Where is shelter? Where is a mate? How to defend?" And the man is also doing the same business, in different ways.

So this struggle for existence is going on, life after life. Even a small insect is engaging in the same struggle—*āhāra-nidrā-bhaya-maithunam*—eating, sleeping, defending, and mating. Bird, beast, insect, fish—everywhere the same struggle: "Where is food? Where is sex? Where is shelter? How to defend?" So the *śāstra* [scripture] says we have done these things in many, many past lives, and if we don't get out of this struggle for existence, we'll have to do them again in many, many future lives. So these things should be stopped.

Therefore Prahlāda Mahārāja advises his friends [*Śrīmad-Bhāgavatam* 7.6.3],

sukham aindriyakaṁ daityā
deha-yogena dehinām
sarvatra labhyate daivād
yathā duḥkham ayatnataḥ

"My dear friends, material pleasure—which is due simply to this material body—is essentially the same in any body. And just as misery comes without our trying for it, so the happiness we deserve will also come, by higher arrangement." A dog has a material body, and I have a material body. So my sex pleasure and the dog's sex pleasure is the same. Of course, a dog is not afraid of having sex on the street, in front of everyone. We hide it in a nice apartment. That's all. But the activity is the same. There is no difference.

Still, people are taking this sex pleasure between a man and woman in a nice decorated apartment as very advanced. But this is not advanced. And yet they are making a dog's race for this "advancement." Prahlāda Mahārāja says we are imagining that there are different types of pleasure on account of different types of body, but the pleasure is fundamentally the same.

Naturally, according to the different types of body, there are some external differences in the pleasure, but the basic amount and quality of this pleasure has very well defined limitations. That is called destiny. A pig has a certain type of body, and his eatable is stool. This is destined. You cannot change it—"Let the pig eat *halavā*." That is not possible. Because the soul has a particular type of body, he must eat a particular type of food. Can anyone, any scientist, improve the standard of living of a pig? Is it possible? [*Laughter*.]

Therefore Prahlāda Mahārāja says that everything about material pleasure is already fixed. The uncivilized men in the jungle are having the same sex pleasure as the so-called civilized men who boast, "Instead of living in that hut made of leaves, we are living in a skyscraper building. This is advancement."

But Vedic civilization says, "No, this is not advancement. Real advancement is self-realization—how much you have realized your relationship with God."

Sometimes people misunderstand, thinking that sages who try for self-realization are lazy. In a high court a judge is sitting soberly, apparently doing nothing, and he is getting the highest salary. And another man in the same court—he's working hard all day long, rubber-stamping, and he is getting not even one-tenth of the judge's salary. He's thinking, "I am so busy and working so hard, yet I am not getting a good salary. And this man is just sitting on the bench, and he's getting such a fat salary." The criticism of Hinduism as "inhibiting progress" is like that: it comes out of ignorance. The Vedic civilization is for self-realization. It is meant for the intelligent person, the person who will not just work like an ass but who will try for that thing which he did not achieve in so many other lives—namely, self-realization.

For example, we are sometimes labeled "escapists." What is the charge?

Disciple: They say we are escaping from reality.

Śrīla Prabhupāda: Yes, we are escaping *their* reality. But their reality is a dog's race, and our reality is to advance in self-realization, Kṛṣṇa consciousness. That is the difference. Therefore the mundane, materialistic workers have been described as *mūḍhas*, asses. Why? Because the ass works very hard for no tangible gain. He carries on his back tons of cloth for the washerman, and the washerman in return gives him a little morsel of grass. Then the ass stands at the washerman's door, eating the grass, while the washerman loads him up again. The ass has no sense to think, "If I get out of the clutches of this washerman, I can get grass anywhere. Why am I carrying so much?"

The mundane workers are like that. They're busy at the office, very busy. If you want to see the fellow, "I am very busy now." [*Laughter.*] So what is the result of your being so busy? "Well, I take two pieces of toast and one cup of tea. That's all." [*Laughter.*] And for this purpose you are so busy? Or, he is busy all day simply so that in the evening he can look at his account books and say, "Oh, the balance had been one thousand dollars—now it has become two thousand." That is his satisfaction. But still he will have the same two pieces of bread and one cup of tea, even though he has increased his balance from one thousand to two thousand. And still he'll work hard. This is why *karmīs* are called *mūḍhas*. They work like asses, without any real aim of life.

But Vedic civilization is different. The accusation implied in the question is not correct. In the Vedic system, people are not lazy. They are very busy working for a higher purpose. And that busy-ness is so important that Prahlāda Mahārāja says, *kaumāra ācaret prājño:* "Beginning from childhood, one should work for self-realization." One should not lose a second's time. So that is Vedic civilization.

Of course, the materialistic workers—they see, "These men are not working like us, like dogs and asses. So they are escaping."

Yes, escaping your fruitless endeavor.

The Vedic civilization of self-realization begins from the *varṇāśrama* system of social organization. *Varnāśramācāravatā puruṣeṇa paraḥ pumān viṣṇur ārādhyate:* "Everyone should offer up the fruits of his occupational duty to the lotus feet of the Lord Viṣṇu, or Kṛṣṇa." That is why the Vedic system is called *varṇāśrama*—literally, "social organization with a spiritual perspective."

The *varṇāśrama* system has four social and four spiritual divisions. the social divisions are the *brāhmaṇas* [teachers and priests], *kṣatriyas* [administrators and military men], *vaiśyas* [farmers and merchants], and *śūdras* [laborers and craftsmen], while the spiritual divisions are the *brahmacārīs* [students], *gṛhasthas* [householders], *vānaprasthas* [retirees], and *sannyāsīs* [renunciants]. But the ultimate goal is *viṣṇur ārādhyate*—the worship of the Supreme Lord, Viṣṇu, by all. That is the idea.

But the members of the modern so-called civilization do not know of *varṇāśrama*. Therefore they have created a society that is simply a dog's race. The dog is running on four legs, and they are running on four wheels. That's all. And they think the four-wheel race is advancement of civilization.

Vedic civilization is different. As Nārada Muni says, *tasyaiva hetoḥ prayateta kovido na labhyate yad bhramatām upary adhaḥ*: the learned, astute person will use this life to gain what he has missed in countless prior lives—namely, realization of self and realization of God. Someone may ask, "Then shall we do nothing?" Yes do nothing simply to improve your material position. Whatever material happiness is allotted for you by destiny, you'll get it wherever you are. Take to Kṛṣṇa consciousness. You'll get these other things besides.

"How shall I get them?"

How? *Kālena sarvatra gabhīra-raṁhasā:* by the arrangement of eternal time, everything will come about in due course. The example is given that even though you do not want distress, still distress comes upon you. Similarly, even if you do not work hard for the happiness that is destined to be yours, still it will come.

Similarly, Prahlāda Mahārāja says, *na tat-prayāsaḥ kartavyam:* you should not waste your energy for material happiness, because you cannot get more than what you are destined to have. That is not possible. "How can I believe it—that by working harder I will not get more material happiness than I would otherwise have had?"

Because you are undergoing so many distressing conditions even though you do not want them. Who wants distress? For example, in our country, Mahatma Gandhi was killed by his own countrymen. He was a great man, he was protected by so many followers, he was beloved by all—and still he was killed. Destiny. Who can protect you from all these distressing conditions?

"So," you should conclude, "if these distressing conditions come upon me by force, the other kind of condition, the opposite number, will also come. Therefore why shall I waste my time trying to avoid distress and gain so-called happiness? Let me utilize my energy for Kṛṣṇa consciousness." That is intelligence. You cannot check your destiny. The magazine's question touches on this point.

Puṣṭa Kṛṣṇa: Yes, the usual charge is that this Vedic system of civilization is fatalistic, and that as a result people are not making as much material progress as they otherwise would.

Śrīla Prabhupāda: No, no, the Vedic system is not fatalistic. It is fatalistic only in the sense that one's *material* destiny cannot be changed. But your spiritual life is in your hands. Our point is this: The whole Vedic civilization is based on the understanding that destiny allows only a certain amount of material happiness in this world, and that our efforts should therefore be directed toward self-realization. Nobody is enjoying uninterrupted material happiness. That is not possible. A certain amount of material happiness and a certain amount of material distress—these both must be present always. So just as you cannot check your distressing condition of life, similarly you cannot check your happy condition of life. It will come automatically. Therefore, don't waste your time with these things. Better you utilize your energy for advancing in Kṛṣṇa consciousness.

Puṣṭa Kṛṣṇa: So then, Śrīla Prabhupāda, would it be accurate, after all, to say that people who have this Vedic conception would not try for progress?

Śrīla Prabhupāda: No, no. "Progress"—first you must understand what actual progress is. The thing is that if you try to progress vainly, what is the use of trying? If it is a fact you cannot change your material destiny, why should you try for that? Rather, whatever energy you have, utilize it for understanding Kṛṣṇa consciousness. That is real progress. Make your spiritual understanding—your understanding of God and self—perfectly clear.

For instance, in our International Society for Krishna Consciousness, our main business is how to make advancement in Kṛṣṇa consciousness. We are not enthusiastic about opening big, big factories with big, big money-earning machines. No. We are satisfied with whatever material happiness and distress we are destined. But we are very eager to utilize our energy for progressing in Kṛṣṇa consciousness. This is the point.

So the Vedic system of civilization is meant for realizing God: *viṣṇur ārādhyate*. In the Vedic system, people try for that. Actually, the followers of *varṇāśrama-dharma*, they never tried for economic development. You'll find in India, still, millions of people taking bath in the Ganges during Kumbha-melā. Have you have been to the Kumbha-melā festival?

Disciple: No.

Śrīla Prabhupāda: At the Kumbha-melā, millions of people come to take bath in the Ganges because they are interested in how to become spiritually liberated from this material world. They're not lazy. They travel thousands of miles to take bath in the Ganges at the holy place of Prayag. So although they are not busy in the dog's race, these people are not lazy. *Yā niśā sarva-bhūtānāṁ tasyāṁ jāgarti saṁyamī*: "What is night for ordinary beings is the time of wakefulness for the self-controlled." The self-controlled man wakes up very early—practically in the middle of the night—and works for spiritual realization while others are sleeping. Similarly, during the daytime the dogs and asses think, "We are working, but these spiritualists, they are not working."

So there are two different platforms, the material and the spiritual. Followers of the Vedic civilization, which is practiced in India—although nowadays it is distorted—actually, these people are not lazy. They are very, very busy. Not only very, very busy, but also *kaumāra ācaret prājño dharmān bhāgavatān iha:* they are trying to become self-realized from the very beginning of life. They are so busy that they want to begin the busyness from their very childhood. Therefore it is wrong to think they are lazy.

People who accuse followers of Vedic civilization of laziness or of "inhibiting progress" do not know what real progress is. The Vedic civilization is not interested in the false progress of economic development. For instance, sometimes people boast, "We have gone from the hut to the skyscraper." They think this is progress. But in the Vedic system of civilization, one thinks about how much he is advanced in self-realization. He may live in a hut and become very advanced in self-realization. But if he wastes his time turning his hut into a skyscraper, then his whole life is wasted, finished. And in his next life he is going to be a dog, although he does not know it. That's all.

Puṣṭa Kṛṣṇa: Śrīla Prabhupāda, then this question may be raised: If destiny cannot be checked, then why not, when a child is born, simply let him run around like an animal? And whatever happens to him . . .

Śrīla Prabhupāda: No. That is the advantage of this human form of life. You can train the child spiritually. That is possible. Therefore it is said, *tasyaiva hetoḥ prayateta kovido:* use this priceless human form to attain what you could not attain in so many millions of lower forms. For that spiritual purpose you should engage your energy. That advantage is open to you now, in the human form. *Ahaituky apratihatā:* pure devotional service to the Lord, Kṛṣṇa consciousness, is open to you now, and it cannot be checked. Just as your advancement of so-called material happiness is already destined and cannot be checked, similarly, your advancement in spiritual life cannot be checked—if you endeavor for it. No one can check your spiritual advancement. Try to understand this.

Puṣṭa Kṛṣṇa: So, then, we can't say that the Vedic system, or *sanātana-dharma*, is fatalistic. There actually is endeavor for progress.

Śrīla Prabhupāda: Certainly—spiritual progress. As for the question of "fatalistic," I have often given this example: Let us say a man is condemned by a court of law to be hanged. Nobody can check it. Even the same judge who gave the verdict cannot check it. But if the man begs for the mercy of the king, the king can check the execution. He can go totally above the law. Therefore the *Brahma-saṁhitā* [5.54] says, *karmāṇi nirdahati kintu ca bhakti-bhājām:* destiny can be changed by Kṛṣṇa for His devotees; otherwise it is not possible.

Therefore our only business should be to surrender to Kṛṣṇa. And if you artificially want to be more happy by economic development, that is not possible.

Puṣṭa Kṛṣṇa: Question number three?

Śrīla Prabhupāda: Hm? No. First of all make sure that everything is clear. Why are you so eager to progress? [*Laughter.*]

Try to understand what is what. The first thing is that your destiny cannot be changed. That's a fact. But in spite of your destiny, if you try for Kṛṣṇa consciousness, you can achieve spiritual success. Otherwise, why did Prahlāda Mahārāja urge his friends, *kaumāra ācaret:* "Take up Kṛṣṇa consciousness from your very childhood"? If destiny cannot be changed, then why was Prahlāda Mahārāja urging this? Generally, "destiny" means your material future. That you cannot change. But even that can be changed when you are in spiritual life.

Puṣṭa Kṛṣṇa: What is the meaning of *apratihatā?* You

said that spiritual development cannot be checked.

Śrīla Prabhupāda: *Apratihatā* means this: Suppose you are destined to suffer. So *apratihatā* means that in spite of your so-called destiny to suffer, if you take to Kṛṣṇa consciousness your suffering will be reduced, or there will be no suffering—and in spite of any suffering, you can make progress in spiritual life. Just like Prahlāda Mahārāja himself. His father put him into so many suffering conditions, but he was not impeded—he made spiritual progress. He didn't care about his father's attempts to make him suffer. That state of existence is called *apratihatā:* if you want to execute Kṛṣṇa consciousness, your material condition of life cannot check it. That is the real platform of progress.

Of course, insofar as your material condition is concerned, generally that cannot be checked. You have to suffer. But in the case of a devotee, that suffering also can be stopped or minimized. Otherwise, Kṛṣṇa's statement would be false: *ahaṁ tvāṁ sarva-pāpebhyo mokṣayiṣyāmi*—"I will deliver you from all the reactions to your sinful activities." Suffering must befall me on account of my sinful activities, but Kṛṣṇa says, "I will deliver you from all the reactions to your sinful activities." This should be clear. Ordinarily, destiny cannot be checked. Therefore, instead of wasting your time trying to change your economic condition or material destiny apart from Kṛṣṇa consciousness, you should employ your priceless human energy for attaining Kṛṣṇa consciousness, which cannot be checked.

We see so many men working so hard. Does this mean that every one of them will become a Ford, a

Rockefeller? Why not? Everyone is trying his best. But Mr. Ford was destined to become a rich man. His destiny was there, and so he became a rich man. Another man may work just as hard as Ford, but this does not mean he will become as rich as Ford. This is practical. You cannot change your destiny simply by working hard like asses and dogs. No. But you can utilize your special human energy for improving your Kṛṣṇa consciousness. That's a fact.

Disciple: Śrīla Prabhupāda, if destiny cannot be changed, what does Kṛṣṇa mean when He says, "Be thou happy by this sacrifice"?

Śrīla Prabhupāda: Do you know what is meant by "sacrifice"?

Disciple: Sacrifice to Viṣṇu, to Kṛṣṇa.

Śrīla Prabhupāda: Yes. That means pleasing Kṛṣṇa. If Kṛṣṇa is pleased, He can change destiny. *Karmāṇi nirdahati kintu ca bhakti-bhājām*: for those who serve Him with love and devotion, Kṛṣṇa can change destiny. So sacrifice, *yajña,* means pleasing Kṛṣṇa. Our whole Kṛṣṇa consciousness movement means pleasing Kṛṣṇa. That is the whole program. In all other business, there is no question of pleasing Kṛṣṇa. When one nation declares war upon another, there is no question of pleasing Kṛṣṇa or serving Kṛṣṇa. They're pleasing their own senses, serving their own whims. When the First and Second World Wars began, it was not for pleasing Kṛṣṇa. The Germans wanted that their sense gratification not be hampered by the Britishers. That means it was a war of sense gratification. "The Britishers are achieving their sense gratification; we cannot. All right, fight." So there was no question of pleasing Kṛṣṇa. Hm. Next question?

CONCOCTED RELIGION

Pusta Kṛṣṇa: Question number three. "It is said that the greatest strength of Hinduism is its catholicity, or breadth of outlook, but that this is also its greatest weakness, in that there are very few common prescribed religious observances which are obligatory for all, as in other religions. Is it necessary and possible to outline certain basic minimum observances for all Hindus?"

Śrīla Prabhupāda: So far as the Vedic religion is concerned, it is not simply for the so-called Hindus. That is to be understood. This is *sanātana-dharma*, the eternal and universal nature and duty of every living being. It is for all living entities, all living beings. That is why it is called *sanātana-dharma*. The living entity is *sanātana*, or eternal; God is *sanātana*; and there is *sanātana-dhāma*, the Lord's eternal abode. As Kṛṣṇa describes in the Bhagavad-gītā [8.20], *paras tasmāt tu bhāvo 'nyo vyakto 'vyaktāt sanātanaḥ*: "Yet there is another unmanifest nature, which is eternal." And in the Eleventh Chapter Kṛṣṇa Himself is described as *sanātanaḥ*. Do you remember? He is described as *sanātanaḥ*, the supreme eternal.

So actually, the Vedic system is called *sanātana-dharma*, not Hindu *dharma*. This is a wrong conception. This *sanātana-dharma* is meant for all living entities, not just the so-called Hindus. The very term "Hindu" is a misconception. The Muslims referred to the Indian people, who lived on the other side of the river Sind, as "Sindus"—actually, due to the peculiarities of pronunciation, as "Hindus." In any case, the Muslims called

India "Hindustan," which means "the land on the other side of the river Sind, or 'Hind.'" Otherwise, "Hindustan" has no Vedic reference. So this "Hindu *dharma*" has no Vedic reference.

The real Vedic *dharma* is *sanātana-dharma*, or *varṇāśrama-dharma*. First of all, one has to understand this. Now that *sanātana-dharma*, or Vedic *dharma*, is being disobeyed, distorted, and misrepresented, it has come to be misunderstood as "Hinduism." That is a fake understanding. That is not the real understanding. We have to study *sanātana-dharma*, or *varṇāśrama-dharma*. Then we'll understand what the Vedic religion is.

Every living entity is eternal, *sanātana*. God is also eternal, and we can live with God in His *sanātana-dhāma*, His eternal abode. This reciprocation is called *sanātana-dharma*, the eternal nature and duty of the living being. So Vedic religion means this *sanātana-dharma*, not "Hindu *dharma*." Read the verse from *Bhagavad-gītā* that describes Kṛṣṇa as *sanātanaḥ*.

Rādhā-vallabha:

tvam akṣaraṁ paramaṁ veditavyaṁ
tvam asya viśvasya paraṁ nidhānam
tvam avyayaḥ śāśvata-dharma-goptā
sanātanas tvaṁ puruṣo mato me

"You are the supreme primal objective. You are the ultimate resting place of this universe. You are inexhaustible, and You are the supreme eternal. You are the maintainer of the eternal religion, the Personality of Godhead. This is my opinion." [*Bhagavad-gītā* 11.18]

Śrīla Prabhupāda: This understanding is wanted. Kṛṣṇa is eternal, we are eternal, and the place where we will live with Him and exchange our feelings—that is eternal. And the system which teaches this eternal system of reciprocation—that is called *sanātana-dharma*, the eternal religion. It is meant for everyone.

Puṣṭa Kṛṣṇa: How can people follow *sanātana-dharma* on a practical, daily basis?

Śrīla Prabhupāda: How are we doing it? Is it not practical? Kṛṣṇa requests, *man-manā bhava mad-bhakto mad-yājī māṁ namaskuru:* "Always think of Me, become My devotee, worship Me, and offer your obeisances to Me." Where is the impracticality? Where is the difficulty? And Kṛṣṇa promises, *mām evaiṣyasy asaṁśaya:* "If you do this, you'll come to Me. Without any doubt you'll come to Me." Why don't you do that?

Later Kṛṣṇa requests, *sarva-dharmān parityajya mām ekaṁ śaraṇaṁ vraja:* "Give up all varieties of concocted religion and simply surrender to Me." This is practical religion. Just surrender to Kṛṣṇa and think, "I am a devotee of Kṛṣṇa, a servant of Kṛṣṇa." Take this simple approach. Then everything will be immediately done. Real *dharma*, real religion, means *dharmaṁ tu sākṣād bhagavat-praṇītam:* what God says, that is *dharma*. Now, God says, "give up all this concocted *dharma* and just surrender unto Me." So take that *dharma*.

Why don't you take Kṛṣṇa's instruction? Why do you go outside His instruction? That is the cause of all your troubles. You do not know the difference between this *sanātana-dharma*, the real, eternal religion, and your concocted *dharma*. If you take to some false religious system, then you suffer. But if you take to the real religious system, then you'll be happy.

Of course, nowadays India, like the rest of the world, has also given up the real religious system—*sanātana-dharma*, or *varṇāśrama-dharma*. In India they have accepted a hodgepodge thing called "Hinduism." So there is trouble. Everywhere, but in India especially, people should know that the real religion is this Vedic system. Vedic religion means *varṇāśrama-dharma*. Kṛṣṇa says—God says—*cātur-varṇyaṁ mayā sṛṣṭam*: "For spiritual and material progress, the four occupational divisions of society have been set up by Me." So that is obligatory, just as the state law is obligatory. You cannot say, "I don't accept this law." No. You have to accept it if you want to have a happy life. You cannot become an outlaw. Then you'll not be happy. You'll be punished.

Now, God says, *mayā sṛṣṭam*: "This *varṇāśrama* system is given by Me." So how can we refuse to follow it? that means we are denying the real religion. *Dharmaṁ tu sākṣād bhagavat-praṇītam*: real *dharma*, real religion, means the order given by God. And God says, *cātur-varṇyaṁ mayā sṛṣṭaṁ guṇa-karma-vibhāgaśaḥ*: "For the proper management of human society, I have created these four social divisions, based on people's qualities and actions." So you have to accept it.

Puṣṭa Kṛṣṇa: This would be the prescription for all people?

Śrīla Prabhupāda: For everyone. At the head of the social body there must be the intelligent class of men, who will give advice; then there must be the administrative and protective class, the farming and mercantile class, and the laboring class. This is all given in the *Bhagavad-gītā: brāhmaṇa, kṣatriya, vaiśya, śūdra.*

But when you fully surrender to Kṛṣṇa, you can give up all the regulations pertaining to these four social classes. That is why Kṛṣṇa says, *sarva-dharmān parityajya:* "In the ultimate issue, My instruction is to give up all religious formularies"—including even Vedic formularies—"and simply surrender to Me." "*Brāhmaṇa-dharma,*" "*kṣatriya-dharma,*" "Hindu *dharma,*" this *dharma,* that *dharma*—give all these up and simply surrender to Kṛṣṇa, because the ultimate aim of *dharma* is to come to Kṛṣṇa. "You directly come to Me; then everything is all right."

Disciple: So many people concoct their own system and say, "This is the way to go to God."

Śrīla Prabhupāda: Then let them suffer. What can be done? If you don't accept the laws of the state and you manufacture your own laws, then you'll suffer. The state says, "Keep to the right." But if you make your own law—"No, I will keep to the left"—then you'll suffer. It's a fact.

Kṛṣṇa is personally advising: *sarva-dharmān parityajya mam ekaṁ śaraṇaṁ vraja:* "Give up all your concocted religions and surrender to Me alone." take His advice and be happy.

CASTE SYSTEM CAST OUT

Puṣṭa Kṛṣṇa: Next question, Śrīla Prabhupāda. "Will the fundamental values of the Vedic religion be in any way affected by the eradication of the caste system, toward which a concerted effort is now being made at all levels?"

Śrīla Prabhupāda: The Vedic system of religion we have been describing—the *varṇāśrama* system created by Kṛṣṇa—is not to be confused with the present-day caste system—determination of social divisions by birth. But as to eradication of all social divisions, it cannot be done. This is still more foolishness, because Kṛṣṇa Himself says, *cātur-varṇyaṁ mayā sṛṣṭaṁ guṇa-karma-vibhāgaśaḥ:* "This system of four social divisions, according to quality and work, is ordained by Me." But the difficulty is that this so-called caste system has come in, on account of the false notion that in order to be a *brāhmaṇa*, one must be the son of a *brāhmaṇa*. That is the caste system. But Kṛṣṇa does not say that. He says "according to quality and work." He never says "according to birth." So this so-called caste system in India is a false notion of *cātur-varṇyaṁ*, the system of four social divisions. The real system of *cātur-varṇyaṁ* means *guṇa-karma-vibhāgaśaḥ*, determination of the four social divisions according to quality and work. One must be qualified.

And how does one become qualified? That is also described. For instance, in *Bhagavad-gītā* Kṛṣṇa describes the qualities of a *brāhmaṇa* as follows: *śamo damas tapaḥ śaucaṁ kṣāntir ārjavam eva ca jñānaṁ vijñānam āstikyam*. "Peacefulness, self-control, austerity, purity, tolerance, honesty, knowledge, wisdom, and religiousness." So people who want to become *brāhmaṇas* must be educated to acquire these qualities. It is not enough simply to abolish the caste system, which is contaminated by the false conception of qualification by birthright. Certainly, this wrong caste system should be abolished.

Also, educational centers should be opened for teaching people how to become genuine *brāhmaṇas* and *kṣatriyas*. *Guṇa-karma-vibhāgaśaḥ:* according to their qualities and work, people naturally belong to different social groupings. So you cannot avoid it, but because you have created a false caste system, that should be abolished, and the system recommended by Kṛṣṇa—that should be adopted.

In any event, you cannot avoid the natural occurrence of various social divisions. Nature's caste system will remain. Take, for example, the brahminical quality of truthfulness. All over the world, wherever you go, you'll find at least one person who is truthful. Does anyone say, "Oh, his father was truthful—therefore, he is truthful"? This is nonsense. Kṛṣṇa never says anything like this. The father may be Hiraṇyakaśipu, a big demon, but his son can still be Prahlāda, a great devotee of the Lord. It is not that one will inevitably become exactly like one's father. Of course, it may be; there is every possibility. But still it is not a fact that the son unavoidably becomes like the father.

Our point is, wherever you go, you'll find a first-class man who is truthful. Now, wherever you find a truthful man, you can classify him as a *brāhmaṇa* and train him to serve the social body in that capacity, as a spiritual teacher and advisor. That is wanted. Why assume, "Here is the son of a truthful man; therefore he is truthful, a *brāhmaṇa*"? That is a misconception. You have to find the truthful men all over the world and train them as *brāhmaṇas*. That we are doing. "If you follow these principles—no illicit sex, no intoxication, no gambling, no meat-eating—you are a *brahmana*. Come on and receive further training." The fellow's father may be a meat-eater or a gambler or a drunkard, but if he himself is truthful and agreeable to the brahminical life, then tell him, "All right, come on—you are welcome." Then everything will be all right.

You could not abolish the truthful class of men even if you wanted to. You'll find truthful men everywhere. You simply have to train them. So Kṛṣṇa says, *cātur-varṇyaṁ mayā sṛṣṭaṁ guṇa-karma-vibhāgaśaḥ*: according to their qualities and work, you take some men and put them in the brahminical class, others in the *kṣatriya* class, still others in the *vaiśya* class, and the rest in the *śūdra* class. But you cannot abolish that system. That is a false attempt.

Puṣṭa Kṛṣṇa: You're saying the natural system is to classify a person and train him for a particular duty, according to his particular inner qualities and his particular propensity to act.

Śrīla Prabhupāda: Yes. That classification is wanted. That must be there.

Puṣṭa Kṛṣṇa: And what will be the benefit of classifying and training people according to their own qualities and propensities?

Śrīla Prabhupāda: The benefit will be that the whole social body will function harmoniously. The social body must have a brain and arms and a belly and legs to be complete. If there is no brain, no head, then what is the use of these arms and legs and belly? It is all dead. So in human society, if there is not a class of learned, truthful, and honest men—men with all the brahminical qualifications—then society is ruined. That is why people are perplexed. Today almost everyone is trained to be a *śūdra*, a laborer: "Go to the factory." That's all. "Go to the factory and get money." And when the man gets some money, he immediately purchases wine and women. So if you try to make society classless, you'll produce such men—useless men, disturbing to the social body. You cannot make society classless. If you try to make it classless, naturally people will all be *śūdras*, fourth-class men, and worse. Then there will be social chaos.

Puṣṭa Kṛṣṇa: But can all people take an equal interest in religion, despite their belonging to different social classifications?

Śrīla Prabhupāda: Yes. This I have already explained, that any civilized human being—he has got some religion. Now, the basic principles of religion are the statements made by God. So here in the Vedic system is what God says. If you take to this system, then the social body will be perfect, not only for Hindus but also for Christians, for Muhammadans, for everyone. And that is being practically realized in our Kṛṣṇa consciousness movement. We have got devotees from all groups of human society, and they are taking to this Vedic system. It is practical. There is no difficulty. So Hindus, Muslims, Christians—everyone should take to this Kṛṣṇa religion and become "Krishnites," "Krishnians." [*Laughter*.] The Greek word *Christo* comes from the Sanskrit *Krishna*. In fact, another spelling of *Krishna* is *Krishta*. So actually, if we take the root meaning, "Christian" means "Krishtian" or "Krishnian." So that is a controversial point, but everyone can take to Kṛṣṇa. Then everything will be settled up.

Puṣṭa Kṛṣṇa: Would you like to hear another question, Śrīla Prabhupāda?
Śrīla Prabhupāda: Yes.
Puṣṭa Kṛṣṇa: "It is said that whereas the *śrutis* [the four original *Vedas*, the *upanisads*, and the *Vedānta-sūtra*] embody eternal truths, the *smṛtis* [the *Purāṇas*, the *Mahābhārata*, the *Rāmāyaṇa*, and corollary Vedic literature] embody the rules of conduct and thus need to be revised according to the dictates of the changing times. Will such a view be acceptable to all sections of society, and if so, how can the new *smṛtis* come into being, and who will give them sanction and sanctity?"
Śrīla Prabhupāda: The *smṛtis* are given by the Lord and His representatives. They come from spiritual authorities such as Lord Caitanya Mahāprabhu. The *śāstra*, or scripture, also gives this authority. For instance, for this age, Kali-yuga, the Lord has prescribed a special means of God-realization—the chanting of His holy name. *Smṛtis* such as the *Bṛhan-nāradīya Purāṇa* say the same thing—that in this age of Kali-yuga, the only possible means of God-realization is chanting the Lord's name. In the *Bhāgavata Purāṇa* [12.3.51] also, Śukadeva Gosvāmī directs,

kaler doṣa-nidhe rājann
asti hy eko mahān guṇaḥ
kīrtanād eva kṛṣṇasya
mukta-saṅgaḥ paraṁ vrajet

"Although in this age there are so many faults—it is truly an ocean of faults—still, there is one very great advantage: simply by chanting the Hare Kṛṣṇa *mantra*, one becomes fully purified and is liberated from all material miseries." So this *smṛti* injunction we should take up, and actually we see all over the world how it is purifying all sections of people. Take to this chanting of Hare Kṛṣṇa; then *śruti*, *smṛti*, everything will be fulfilled. This is the easiest method. *Kīrtanād eva kṛṣṇasya mukta-saṅgaḥ paraṁ vrajet*: chant the Lord's holy name and you'll be liberated.

Puṣṭa Kṛṣṇa: So the *śrutis* are eternally relevant and constant?

Śrīla Prabhupāda: Yes, everything is based on the *śrutis*. as the *Vedānta-sūtra* says, *anāvṛttiḥ śabdāt*: simply by chanting the Lord's names and instructions—His sound vibration—one becomes spiritually realized. *Śabda brahman* means "spiritual sound vibration," and as the *Vedānta-sūtra* instructs us, by chanting this spiritual sound vibration—the instructions and holy name of the Lord—one can become liberated.

Puṣṭa Kṛṣṇa: Also, the *smṛtis* are directly based on the original *śrutis*?

Śrīla Prabhupāda: Yes, for instance, *Bhagavad-gītā* is considered *smṛti*. And *Bhagavad-gītā* also says, *satataṁ kīrtayanto māṁ yatantaś ca dṛḍha-vratāḥ*: "Fully endeavoring with determination, the great souls are always chanting My glories." And as the *Bhakti-rasāmṛta-sindhu*, which is also considered *smṛti*, explains: *śruti-smṛti-purāṇādi*—the great devotees heed both the *śrutis* and the *smṛtis*. Another *smṛti*, *Bṛhan-nāradīya Purāṇa*, enjoins, *harer nāma harer nāma harer nāmaiva kevalam*: "In this age of quarrel, the only way to realize the Lord is to chant

His holy name, chant His holy name, chant His holy name." So because He was in the role of a great devotee, Lord Caitanya followed these injunctions of *śruti* and *smṛti*. *Kṛṣṇa-varṇaṁ tviṣākṛṣṇaṁ sāṅgopāṅgāstra-pārṣadam*. *Kṛṣṇaṁ varṇayati*: Lord Caitanya was always chanting Hare Kṛṣṇa. These examples are evidence that the *smṛtis* are directly based on the *śrutis*. So introduce this Hare Kṛṣṇa *mahā-mantra*. Everyone will be purified.

Puṣṭa Kṛṣṇa: Is *smṛti* more than just rules of conduct?

Śrīla Prabhupāda: Yes. Here is what *smṛti* means:

The four original *Vedas* are considered *śruti*. But simply by hearing them, one cannot understand fully. Therefore, the *smṛtis* have explained further. *Purayati iti purāṇa*: by hearing the *Purāṇas* and other *smṛtis*, one makes his understanding complete. The Vedic *mantras* are not always understood. For instance, the *Vedānta*, which is *śruti*, begins with the *mantra janmādy asya yataḥ*: "The Supreme is that being from whom everything has emanated." This is very abbreviated. But the *Śrīmad-Bhāgavatam*, which is *smṛti*, explains, *janmādy asya yato 'nvayād itaratas cārtheṣv abhijñāh sva-rāt*: "The Supreme Being, from whom everything has emanated, is directly and indirectly cognizant of everything and is fully independent." In this way the *smṛti* explains the *śruti*.

So whether you take *śruti* or *smṛti*, the subject matter is the same. Both *śruti* and *smṛti* are spiritual evidence. We cannot do without either of them. As Śrīla Rūpa Gosvāmī says in the *Bhakti-rasāmṛta-sindhu* [1.2.101],

śruti-smṛti-purāṇādi-
pañcarātra-vidhiṁ vinā
aikāntiki harer bhaktir
utpātāyaiva kalpate

You cannot become purified or actually God conscious without reference to both *śruti* and *smṛti*. So as we push on this Kṛṣṇa consciousness movement, it is not whimsical. It is based on *śruti*, *smṛti*, and *pañcarātriki-vidhi*, the principles of *śruti*, *smṛti*, and the *Nārada-pañcarātra*. Therefore, it is becoming effective.

Puṣṭa Kṛṣṇa: Nevertheless, Śrīla Prabhupāda, the question asks, "Do the *smṛtis* need to be revised according to the changing times?"

Śrīla Prabhupāda: They cannot be changed.

Puṣṭa Kṛṣṇa: The *smṛtis* cannot be changed?

Śrīla Prabhupāda: Nothing can be changed. But according to the time, you have to apply the principles properly. For instance, in Kali-yuga the *smṛti* order is *kīrtanād eva kṛṣṇasya mukta-saṅgaḥ paraṁ vrajet*: to obtain spiritual liberation, one must chant the holy name of the Lord, Hare Kṛṣṇa. So you have to do this. For instance, a doctor may order, "In the morning, take this medicine; in the evening, take that medicine." It is not a change of the doctor's orders. It is simply that according to the time, the doctor's orders call for a particular medicine. But the particular medicine is recommended by the doctor, not by your whims. *Śruti* and *smṛti* cannot be changed, but they may recommend a particular process at a particular time. So there must be adherence to both *śruti* and *smṛti*—to scriptural authority. You cannot modify.

Puṣṭa Kṛṣṇa: There is no question, then, of—as the magazine puts it—"new *smṛti*."

Śrīla Prabhupāda: No. New *smṛti*? they may take it as "new *smṛti*," but *smṛti* is *smṛti*—it is not new. In any spiritual statement, you have to give references to *śruti* and *smṛti*. Otherwise, it is not valid. There must be *veda-pramāṇa, śabda-pramāṇa:* evidence from the *Vedas* and from the explanatory Vedic literature. Otherwise, there is no evidence. Your statement is not valid: you cannot change the original *śruti-smṛti*. But you have to take their particular recommendation for the particular time, just as Kṛṣṇa Caitanya Mahāprabhu did when He urged His followers to heed the injunction of *Bṛhan-nāradīya Purāṇa* [3.8.126]:

harer nāma harer nāma harer nāmaiva kevalam
kalau nāsty eva nāsty eva nāsty eva gatir anyathā

"Chant the holy name, chant the holy name, chant the holy name of Kṛṣṇa. In the present age of quarrel and anxiety, there is no other way to attain God realization, no other way, no other way." So *śruti-smṛti-pramāṇa*—citing evidence from the *Vedas* and the corollary literature—is the only method for making a spiritual statement. You have to take it.

Puṣṭa Kṛṣṇa: Can anyone change . . .

Śrīla Prabhupāda: No!

Puṣṭa Kṛṣṇa: . . . the rules of conduct as described in the *smṛtis*?

Śrīla Prabhupāda: Nobody can change them. But these particular rules and regulations in *śruti-smṛti* are for particular times, particular circumstances. So we have to take these rules and regulations. You cannot change them.

Puṣṭa Kṛṣṇa: And who will sanction a particular application for a particular time and place?

Śrīla Prabhupāda: Yes. This was done by Lord Śrī Kṛṣṇa

Caitanya. When he appeared five hundred years ago, he sanctioned the application of *śruti-smṛti* because He's a genuine authority. He's a genuine *ācārya*. And we are following in the footsteps of Caitanya Mahāprabhu. It is not whimsical. You have to follow the authority in all circumstances.

Puṣṭa Kṛṣṇa: Is this Vedic religion, this *sanātana-dharma*, so broad that everyone is included?

Śrīla Prabhupāda: Yes. *Sanātana* means "eternal." As Kṛṣṇa says in the *Bhagavad-gītā, na hanyate hanyamāne śarīre:* "The living entity within the body is not destroyed when the body is destroyed, because he is eternal." So that eternality belongs to everyone. Not that the Hindus, after giving up this body, exist, and the Muslims or Christians do not exist. Everyone exists eternally. So *sanātana-dharma* is meant for everyone.

Puṣṭa Kṛṣṇa: Then is there anyone actually outside of *sanātana-dharma*?

Śrīla Prabhupāda: Nobody is actually outside. Everyone is an eternal spirit soul, and therefore everyone is meant for the eternal religion, *sanātana-dharma*. You may think that you are not an eternal spirit soul, but that is simply illusion. There are so many rascals who think that with the death of the body, everything is finished. They may think so, but that is not a fact. Similarly, you may think, "I am not a *sanātana-dharmī*—a follower of *sanātana-dharma*—I am a Christian," but actually you are a *sanātana-dharmī*. Of course, if you wish to think otherwise, you can. Who can check it?

Hari-śauri: So whether one can be accepted as following *sanātana-dharma* depends on how one acts?

Śrīla Prabhupāda: Yes. If one does not act accord to the rules and regulations of *sanātana-dharma,* that is his business. That's all.

THE ULTIMATE KNOWLEDGE

Puṣṭa Kṛṣṇa: Śrīla Prabhupāda, this is the next question: "In the Kali-yuga, the current age of quarrel and hypocrisy, *bhakti* [devotional service to the Lord] has been described as the most suitable and easiest of paths for God realization. Yet how is it that Vedantic teachings, with their accent on *jñāna* [cultivation of knowledge], are being given the pride of place by noted savants?"

Śrīla Prabhupāda: The so-called Vedantists, the Māyāvādīs [impersonalists], are bluffers. They do not know what *Vedānta* is. But people want to be bluffed, and the bluffers take advantage of it. The two words combined in the word *Vedānta* are *veda* and *anta. Veda* means "knowledge," and *anta* means "goal" or "end." so *Vedānta* means "the end of all knowledge, or *veda.*" Now, in the *Bhagavad-gītā* Lord Kṛṣṇa says, *vedaiś ca sarvair aham eva vedyaḥ:* "By all the *Vedas* I am to be known." So the whole *Vedānta-sūtra* is a description of the Supreme Personality of Godhead.

The first statement in the *Vedānta-sūtra* is *athāto brahma-jijñāsā:* "Now, having attained a human birth, one should inquire into Brahman, the Absolute Truth." In a nutshell, Brahman is then described: *janmādy asya yataḥ*—"Brahman is the origin of everything." And in *Bhagavad-gītā* Kṛṣṇa says, *ahaṁ sarvasya prabhavaḥ:* "I am the origin of everything." So, again, the *Vedānta-sūtra* actually describes Kṛṣṇa, the Supreme Personality of Godhead.

Now, because Śrīla Vyāsadeva knew that in this Kali-yuga people would not be able to study *Vedānta-sūtra* nicely on account of a lack of education, he personally wrote a commentary on the *Vedānta-sūtra*. That commentary is *Śrīmad-Bhāgavatam*. *Bhāṣyaṁ brahma-sūtrānām:* the *Śrīmad-Bhāgavatam* is the real commentary on the *Vedānta-sūtra*, written by the author of the *Vedānta-sūtra* himself. The *Vedānta-sūtra* was written by Vyāsadeva, and under the instruction of Nārada, his spiritual master, Vyāsadeva wrote a commentary on it. That is *Śrīmad-Bhāgavatam*.

Śrīmad-Bhāgavatam begins with the same aphorism as the *Vedānta-sūtra: janmādy asya yataḥ*, and continues, *anvayād itarataś cārtheṣv abhijñah svarāt*. So actually, the *Vedānta-sūtra* is explained by the author in *Śrīmad-Bhāgavatam*. But the rascal Māyāvādīs—without understanding *Vedānta-sūtra*, and without reading the natural commentary, *Śrīmad-Bhāgavatam*—are posing themselves as Vedantists. That means they are misguiding people. And because people are not educated, they're accepting these rascals as Vedantists. Really, the Māyāvādī Vedantists—they are bluffers. They are not Vedantists. They do not know anything of the *Vedānta-sūtra*. That is the difficulty. Actually, what is stated in the *Śrīmad-Bhāgavatam*—that is real *Vedānta*.

So, if we take *Śrīmad-Bhāgavatam* as the real explanation of *Vedānta-sūtra*, then we will understand *Vedānta*, the end of knowledge. And if we take shelter of the Māyāvādī Vedantists, the bluffers, then we cannot understand *Vedānta*. People do not know anything, and as a result they can be bluffed and cheated by anyone. Therefore now they should learn from this Kṛṣṇa consciousness movement what *Vedānta* is and what the explanation of *Vedānta-sūtra* is. Then they will be benefited.

If we accept *Śrīmad-Bhāgavatam* as the real commentary on *Vedānta-sūtra*, then we'll find that in the *Śrīmad-Bhāgavatam* it is said, *kaler doṣa-nidhe rājann asti hy eko mahān guṇaḥ*: "In this Kali-yuga, which is an ocean of faults, there is one benediction, one opportunity." What is that? *Kīrtanād eva kṛṣṇasya mukta-saṅgaḥ paraṁ vrajet*: "One can become liberated simply by chanting the Hare Kṛṣṇa *mantra*." This is real *Vedānta*. And actually, this liberation by chanting Hare Kṛṣṇa is happening. But people want to be misguided. And there are so many bluffers to misguide them. What can be done? Vyāsadeva has already given the perfect explanation of *Vedānta-sūtra*—the *Śrīmad-Bhāgavatam*. So let people read the *Śrīmad-Bhāgavatam*; then they will understand what *Vedānta* is.

Puṣṭa Kṛṣṇa: Then are the conclusion of the *Vedānta-sūtra* and the conclusion of *Śrīmad-Bhāgavatam* one and the same—*bhakti*?

Śrīla Prabhupāda: Yes. Find this verse: *Kāmasya nendriya-prītir . . .*

Puṣṭa Kṛṣṇa:

kāmasya nendriya-prītir
lābho jīveta yāvatā
jīvasya tattva-jijñāsā
nārtho yaś ceha karmabhiḥ

"Life's desires should never be directed toward sense gratification. One should desire only a healthy life, or self-preservation, since a human being is meant for inquiry about the About Truth. Nothing else should be the goal of one's works." [*Śrīmad-Bhāgavatam* 1.2.10]

Śrīla Prabhupāda: Yes. This verse of *Śrīmad-Bhāgavatam* proceeds directly from the *Vedānta-sūtra*—*athāto brahma-jijñāsā:* "Now is the time to inquire about the Absolute Truth." Here the very same thing is explained. "Don't be entrapped with these temporary, bodily 'necessities of life'—sense gratification. You must inquire about the Absolute Truth." The next verse of *Śrīmad-Bhāgavatam* explains, *vadanti tat tattva-vidas tattvaṁ yaj jñānam advayam:* "Those who know the Absolute Truth describe Him in this way . . ." *Tattva* means "truth." The truth is explained by the *tattva-vit*, one who knows the truth. How? *Brahmeti paramātmeti bhagavān iti śabdyate:* the Absolute Truth is explained as Brahman, the all-pervading spiritual effulgence; as Paramātmā, the localized Supersoul; or as Bhagavān, the Supreme Lord. Understanding these is what *Vedānta-sūtra* means when it says, *athāto brahma-jijñāsā:* "Now one should learn about the Absolute Truth—what Brahman is, what Paramātmā is, what Bhagavān is. In this way, one should make advancement in his spiritual consciousness."

The Māyāvādī Vedantists follow the impersonal commentary of Śaṅkarācārya, *Śārīraka-bhāṣya*. But there are other commentaries on the *Vedānta-sūtra*. Besides the *Śrīmad-Bhāgavatam*, the natural commentary by the author of *Vedānta-sūtra* himself, there are *Vedānta-bhāṣyas* written by Vaiṣṇava *ācāryas* such as Rāmānujācārya, Madhvācārya, Viṣṇu Swami, and Baladeva

Vidyābhūṣaṇa. Unfortunately, the Māyāvādī Vedantists do not care to read these Vaiṣṇava *Vedānta-bhāṣyas*. They simply read *Śārīraka-bhāṣya* and call themselves Vedantists.

Puṣṭa Kṛṣṇa: Why do the Māyāvādī Vedantists read only one commentary? What is the reason for that?

Śrīla Prabhupāda: The reason is that they want to read something that will confirm their illusion that they are God.

The Māyāvādī Vedantists cheat. Suppose I present some proposition. If it is a misconception, generally there are others also who can say something to clarify this misconception. For instance, in a court of law, there are two lawyers. One lawyer is speaking on one point of the law, the other lawyer is speaking on another point of the law. But if the judge listens to one side only, then how will he make a proper judgement? Similarly, the Vedantists are simply reading the *Śārīraka-bhāṣya*. They are not reading other *bhāṣyas*, such as the *Śrīmad-Bhāgavatam*, which is the natural commentary. And they are cheating people. That's all.

Now, the *Vedānta-sūtra* says, *janmādy asya yataḥ*: "The Absolute Truth is that from which everything emanates." But this needs some explanation. One may ask, "Is that Absolute Truth personal or impersonal?" Therefore in the *Bhagavad-gītā* Kṛṣṇa clearly says, *ahaṁ sarvasya prabhavo mattaḥ sarvaṁ pravartate*: "I am the origin of everything; everything comes from Me." So why don't you Māyāvādī Vedantists take it? Why do you simply remain stuck at the point that the Absolute Truth is that from which everything emanates? When Kṛṣṇa, the Absolute Truth, comes before you and says,

"I am the origin of everything—everything comes from Me," why don't you accept Kṛṣṇa as the Absolute Truth? Why do you take the impersonalist view only, that the Absolute Truth has no form? Here is the Absolute Truth speaking—a person. Why don't you take it?

Of course, if people want to be cheated, then who can stop them? In *Bhagavad-gītā* Kṛṣṇa also says, *vedānta-kṛd . . . eva cāham:* "I am the compiler of *Vedānta*." Why do these rascals not consider who compiled *Vedānta?* Vyāsadeva is the incarnation of Kṛṣṇa. He compiled *Vedānta*. Why do these rascals not consider the original Vedantist, Kṛṣṇa? They approach a Māyāvādī instead. So how will they understand *Vedānta*?

Suppose I have written a book. If you cannot understand something in it, then you should come directly to me for an explanation. That is sensible. Why go to a rascal who has nothing to do with my book? Similarly, some rascal Māyāvādī may claim, "I am a Vedantist," but why should I go to a rascal instead of the real compiler of the *Vedānta-sūtra*?

Those who approach the Māyāvādī Vedantists for knowledge are also rascals. They are willingly being cheated. Let the Māyāvādī Vedantists and their followers accept the conclusions of *Bhagavad-gītā* and *Śrīmad-Bhāgavatam*. Then they will understand *Vedānta-sūtra*. They'll be real Vedantists. Otherwise, they will remain cheaters. So if you go to a cheater you'll be cheated, and that is your business.

Puṣṭa Kṛṣṇa: Śrīla Prabhupāda, are you saying that the Māyāvādīs have no knowledge at all?

Śrīla Prabhupāda: Once again, *Vedānta* means "the ultimate knowledge." And what is that knowledge? Kṛṣṇa explains in the *Bhagavad-gītā* [7.19]: *bahūnāṁ janmanām ante jñānavān māṁ prapadyate*. "After many births, one who is actually in knowledge at last surrenders unto Me." So unless one surrenders to Kṛṣṇa, there is no *jñāna*, no knowledge.

Therefore the Māyāvādī Vedantists are all nonsense—they have no knowledge at all. The subject matter of ultimate knowledge, *Vedānta*, is Kṛṣṇa, God. So if one does not know who God is, who Kṛṣṇa is, and if one does not surrender to Him, then where is the question of knowledge? But if a rascal claims that "I am a man of knowledge," what can be done?

In *Bhagavad-gītā* Kṛṣṇa goes on to explain: *vāsudevaḥ sarvam iti sa mahātmā su-durlabhaḥ*. "When one understands that Vāsudeva, Kṛṣṇa, is everything, then that is knowledge. But such a *mahātmā* is very rare." Before coming to this understanding, one has no knowledge. His so-called understanding is simply misunderstanding. *Brahmeti paramātmeti bhagavān iti śabdyate:* one may begin with understanding impersonal Brahman by the speculative method; then, in the secondary stage, one can understand the Paramātmā, the Lord's localized aspect; and the final stage is to understand the Supreme Personality of Godhead, Kṛṣṇa. *Vedaiś ca sarvair aham eva vedyam:* by all the *Vedas*, Kṛṣṇa is to be known. That is the ultimate knowledge. But if you do not understand Kṛṣṇa, then where is your knowledge? Half-way knowledge is not knowledge. It must be complete knowledge.

That complete knowledge is possible, as it is said in the *Bhagavad-gītā, bahūnāṁ janmanām ante*—after many births. Those who are striving to acquire knowledge—after many, many births, when actually by the grace of

God and by the grace of a devotee they come to knowledge, then such persons agree, "Oh, *vāsudevaḥ sarvam iti*: Kṛṣṇa is everything." *Sa mahātmā su-durlabhaḥ*: that *mahātmā*, that great soul, is very rarely to be found. *Durlabhaḥ* means "very rarely found," but the word used is *su-durlabhaḥ*—"very, very rarely to be found." So you cannot easily find such a *mahātmā* who clearly understands Kṛṣṇa.

GETTING SPIRITUAL GUIDANCE

Puṣṭa Kṛṣṇa: May I ask another question, Śrīla Prabhupāda? "Is a *guru* essential for one to enter the spiritual path and attain the goal, and how does one recognize one's *guru*?"

Śrīla Prabhupāda: Yes, a *guru* is necessary. In the *Bhagavad-gītā*, when Kṛṣṇa and Arjuna were talking as friends, there was no conclusion. So Arjuna decided to accept Kṛṣṇa as his *guru*. Find this verse in *Bhagavad-gītā*: *kārpaṇya-doṣopahata-svabhāvaḥ*.

Hari-śauri:

> *kārpaṇya-doṣopahata-svabhāvaḥ*
> *pṛcchāmi tvaṁ dharma-sammūḍha-cetāḥ*
> *yac chreyaḥ syān niścitaṁ brūhi tan me*
> *śiṣyas te 'haṁ śādhi māṁ tvāṁ prapannam*

"[Arjuna said:] Now I am confused about my duty and have lost all composure because of miserly weakness. In this condition I am asking You to tell me for certain what is best for me. Now I am Your disciple, and a soul surrendered unto You. Please instruct me."

Śrīla Prabhupāda: Yes. So a *guru* is necessary. Like Arjuna, everyone is perplexed about his best course of action. Nobody can decide by himself. Even a physician—when he is sick he does not devise his own treatment. He calls for another physician, because his brain is not in order. How can he prescribe the right medicine for himself?

Similarly, when we are perplexed and cannot find any solution, at that time the *guru* is required. It is therefore essential for everyone to surrender to a *guru*, since in our present existence we are all perplexed. Arjuna is representing the perplexed position of the materialistic person. So under the circumstances, a *guru* is required to give us real direction.

Now, Arjuna selected Kṛṣṇa as his *guru*. He did not go to anyone else, because he knew, "I can't find any other means to pacify me. You are the only one." The purport is that like Arjuna, we should also accept Kṛṣṇa as the *guru* who can instruct us in how to get relief from our perplexed position. So Kṛṣṇa is the *guru* not only for Arjuna, but for everyone. If we take instruction from Kṛṣṇa and abide by that instruction, then our life is successful. Conveying that fact is our mission. This Kṛṣṇa consciousness movement teaches, "Accept Kṛṣṇa as your *guru*. Don't divert your attention." We don't say, "I am Kṛṣṇa; follow my order." We never say that. We simply ask people, "Please abide by the order of Kṛṣṇa." Kṛṣṇa says, *sarva-dharmān parityajya mām ekaṁ śaraṇaṁ vraja*, and we say the same thing: "Give up all other ideas of so-called *dharma* and surrender to Kṛṣṇa." The same thing. we don't say of ourselves, "I am the authority." No, we say, "Kṛṣṇa is the authority, and you should surrender to His instruction and try to understand Him." This is the Kṛṣṇa consciousness movement.

Now, one may say, "Kṛṣṇa is no longer present, so how can I surrender to Him?" Kṛṣṇa is no longer present? How can you say that? Kṛṣṇa's instruction is there—*Bhagavad-gītā*. How can you say that Kṛṣṇa is not present? Kṛṣṇa, being absolute, is not different from His words. The words of Kṛṣṇa and Kṛṣṇa Himself—they are the same. That is the meaning of Absolute Truth.

In the relative world, the word *water* and the substance water are different. When I am thirsty, if I simply chant "Water, water, water," my thirst will not be satisfied. I require the real water. That is the nature of the relative world and relative consciousness. But in the spiritual world or spiritual consciousness, the name is the same as the thing that is named. For instance, we are chanting Hare Kṛṣṇa. If Kṛṣṇa were different from the chanting of Hare Kṛṣṇa, then how could we be satisfied chanting the whole day and night? This is the proof. An ordinary name—if you chant "Mr. John, Mr. John," after chanting three times you'll cease. But this Hare Kṛṣṇa *mahā-mantra*—if you go on chanting twenty-four hours a day, you'll never become tired. This is the spiritual nature of the Absolute Truth. This is practical. Anyone can perceive it.

So Kṛṣṇa is present through His words and through His representative. Therefore we advise everyone to accept Kṛṣṇa instructions in *Bhagavad-gītā* and to surrender to His bona fide representative. You have to accept a *guru*, so why go to a pseudo *guru*, who will mislead you? Why not take instructions from a real *guru*? Now you are in doubt about whether a *guru* is needed. Yes, a *guru* is needed, but you have to go to a real *guru*. That is the instruction given by Kṛṣṇa in the *Bhagavad-gītā*. Just find this verse:

tad viddhi praṇipātena
paripraśnena sevayā
upadekṣyanti te jñānaṁ
jñāninas tattva-darśinaḥ

Puṣṭa Kṛṣṇa: "Just try to learn the truth by approaching a spiritual master. Inquire from him submissively and render service unto him. The self-realized soul can impart knowledge unto you because he has seen the truth." [*Bhagavad-gītā* 4.34]

Śrīla Prabhupāda: So this is the real *guru*—one who has seen the truth, just as Arjuna has seen Kṛṣṇa. Arjuna heard Kṛṣṇa's instructions and said, "You are the Absolute Truth." Now, if you take the instruction of Arjuna, then you will understand the Absolute Truth. So what is the instruction of Arjuna? Find out in the tenth chapter.

Puṣṭa Kṛṣṇa:

arjuna uvāca
paraṁ brahma paraṁ dhāma
pavitraṁ paramaṁ bhavān
puruṣaṁ śāśvataṁ divyam
ādi-devam ajaṁ vibhum

"Arjuna said, 'You are the Supreme Personality of Godhead, the ultimate abode, the purest, the Absolute Truth. You are the eternal, transcendental, original person, the unborn, the greatest.'" [*Bhagavad-gītā* 10.12]

Śrīla Prabhupāda: And the *Vedānta-sūtra* says, *athāto brahma-jijñāsā:* "Now, in the human form of life, is the time to inquire into what is the Supreme Brahman." So here in *Bhagavad-gītā* Arjuna has realized, "O Kṛṣṇa, You are the Supreme Brahman." So you should make Arjuna your *guru* and Kṛṣṇa your *guru*. Arjuna is the representative of Kṛṣṇa, the friend of Kṛṣṇa. The *guru* is essential. But why go to a bogus *guru*? You will be cheated. For instance, when you are diseased, for your treatment you need to go to a physician. But you want to go to a real physician, not a cheater who has no knowledge of medical science and misrepresents himself—"I am a physician, an M.D." Then you'll be cheated. The *guru* is necessary; that's a fact. But go to the real *guru*. Who is the real *guru*? The real *guru* is Kṛṣṇa or one who has seen Kṛṣṇa, such as Arjuna.

CIVILIZATION MEANS REGULATION

Puṣṭa Kṛṣṇa: May I ask the next question, Śrīla Prabhupāda? "Are fasting and other dietary regulations necessary for leading a spiritual life?"

Śrīla Prabhupāda: Certainly. For advancement in spiritual life, such *tapasya* is essential. *Tapasya* means voluntarily accepting something which may be painful. For instance, we are recommending no illicit sex, no intoxication, no gambling, no meat-eating. So those who are accustomed to these bad habits—for them, in the beginning it may be a little difficult. But in spite of this difficulty, one has to do it. That is *tapasya*. To rise early in the morning—for those who are not practiced, it is a little painful, but one has to do it. So according to the Vedic injunctions, there are some *tapasyas* that must be done. It is not "I may do it or not do it." These austerities *must* be done. For example, in the *Muṇḍaka Upaniṣad* it is ordered that if one wants to become self-realized, one must approach a spiritual master: *tad-vijñānārthaṁ sa gurum evābhigacchet*. So there is no question of "optional"; it must be done. And one must carry out the order of the spiritual master and the order of the *śāstra*, or scripture. When you follow without consideration of whether it is convenient or inconvenient, simply because it must be done, that is called *tapasya*. *Tapo divyam*: like other great spiritual authorities, Ṛṣabhādeva orders that this human life is meant for austerity aimed toward realizing God. Therefore in our Vedic civilization we find so many rules and regulations.

At the very beginning of life one must be a *brahmacārī*. He must go to the spiritual master's place and act like a menial servant. If the spiritual master says "go and pick up some wood from the forest," one may be a king's son, but he cannot refuse the spiritual master's order. He must go. Even Kṛṣṇa was ordered by His spiritual master to go and pick up some dry wood from the forest. So He had to go. Although His father was Nanda Mahārāja, a village *vaiśya* king, and although Kṛṣṇa was the Personality of Godhead Himself, still He could not refuse. He had to go. *Nicavat*—just like a menial servant. This is *brahmācārya*, spiritual student life. This is *tapasya*. *Tapasya* is so essential that one has to do it. There is no question of an alternative.

After *brahmacārī* life, one may marry. This means he enters *gṛhastha* life, household life. That is also *tapasya*. He cannot have sex whenever he likes. No. The *śāstra* says, "You must have sex like this: once in a month and only for begetting children." So that is also *tapasya*.

People do not follow any *tapasya* at the present moment, but human life is meant for *tapasya*—regulative principles. Even in ordinary affairs—let us say you are driving your car on some urgent business, and you see a red light. You have to stop. You cannot say, "I have to be there in a few minutes. I must go." No. You must stop. That is *tapasya*. So *tapasya* means following the regulative principles strictly, according to the higher order. And that is human life.

Animal life, however, means you can do whatever you like. On the road, animals may keep to the right or keep to the left; it doesn't matter. Their irregularity is not taken as an offense, because they are animals. But if a human being does not follow the regulative principles, he is sinful. He'll be punished. Consider the same example: When there is a red light, if you do not stop you'll be punished. But if a cat or dog transgresses—"Never mind the red light; I shall go"—he's not punished. So *tapasya* is meant for the human being. He must do it if he at all wants to make progress in life. It is essential.

Puṣṭa Kṛṣṇa: And so, Śrīla Prabhupāda, *tapasya* includes dietary regulations?

Śrīla Prabhupāda: That is also *tapasya*. For example, we prohibit meat-eating. So in your country this is a little troublesome. From the very beginning of life, a child is habituated to eating meat. the mother purchases powdered meat and mixes it with liquid and feeds it to the infant. I have seen it. So practically everyone has been brought up eating meat. Yet I say, "Don't eat meat." Therefore that is troublesome. But if one is serious about becoming self-realized, one must accept the order. That is *tapasya*.

Tapasya applies to diet, to personal behavior, to dealings with others, and so on and so forth. In every aspect of life, there is *tapasya*. That is all described in the *Bhagavad-gītā*. Mental *tapasya*. Bodily *tapasya*. Verbal *tapasya*—controlling *vaco-vegam*, the urge to talk loosely or whimsically. You cannot talk nonsense. If you talk, you must talk about Kṛṣṇa. That is *tapasya*. There is also *tapasya* in connection with *krodha-vegam*, the urge to express one's anger. If one becomes angry and wants to express it by beating someone or doing something very violent, *tapasya* will restrict him—"No, don't do it." There is also *tapasya* with regards to the tongue, belly, and genitals. One cannot eat anything and everything, or at any time he pleases. Nor can one have sex freely, but only according to the scriptural injunctions. "I am sexually inclined, but I cannot do it. This is not the time." That is *tapasya*.

So one should practice *tapasya* in every way—in body, mind, words, personal behavior, and dealings with others. That is human life. *Tapo divyam:* if you want to simply be a human being, and especially if you want to make progress in spiritual life, you must act according to the sastric injunctions. That means *tapasya*. Before Brahmā could take part in creation, he had to undergo *tapasya*. Is it not stated in the *śāstra*? Yes. So *tapasya* is essential. You cannot avoid it.

And what is the aim of performing *tapasya*? The aim is to please the Supreme Lord through the spiritual master. *Yasya prasādād bhagavat-prasādo*: "One can attain the mercy of the Lord only by attaining the mercy of the spiritual master." This is the idea.

Now, in today's educational institutions, who is teaching this *tapasya*? Where is the school or college? The students are even smoking in front of their teacher, and it is tolerated. No offense. What can you expect from such students? This is an animal civilization. This is not human civilization. No *tapasya*, no *brahmacārī* life. Real civilization means *tapo divyam*, godly austerity. And this *tapasya* begins with *brahmacārī* life, learning to control the senses—that is the beginning of life. Not "A-B-C-D" learning, and maybe your character is less than an animal's, though you have a degree from the university. "Never mind. You have become a learned man." No—that is not accepted.

Even from the standpoint of basic moral instruction, we must ask: Who today is educated? The educated person is described by Cāṇakya Paṇḍita:

mātṛ-vat para-dāreṣu
para-dravyeṣu loṣṭra-vat
ātma-vat sarva-bhūteṣu
yaḥ paśyati sa paṇḍitāḥ

"The educated man sees another's wife as his mother and another's property as untouchable garbage, and he sees all others as equal to himself." That is the *paṇḍita*, the learned man. In *Bhagavad-gītā* [5.18] Kṛṣṇa also describes the *paṇḍita:*

vidyā-vinaya-sampanne
brāhmaṇe gavi hastini
śuni caiva śva-pāke ca
paṇḍitāḥ sama-darśinaḥ

"The humble sage, by virtue of true knowledge, sees with equal vision a learned and gentle *brāhmaṇa*, a cow, an elephant, a dog, and a dog-eater." That is a learned man. Not this degree-holder. A degree-holder who has no *tapasya* and no character—Kṛṣṇa says he is *māyayāpahṛta-jñānā*, "his knowledge is stolen by illusion." Although he has learned so many things, nonetheless, *māyā* has taken away his knowledge. He's a rascal. He's an animal. This is the perspective of Vedic civilization.

CLEANSING THE HEART

Puṣṭa Kṛṣṇa: Next question, Śrīla Prabhupāda? "What is the role of rituals in religion? Are they to be discouraged, as is being advocated by some reformists, or are they to be encouraged? If so, in what form?"

Śrīla Prabhupāda: A ritual is a practice based on *tapasya*, or austerity. Generally, unless one undergoes the ritualistic ceremonies for purification, he remains unclean. But in this age, because it is practically impossible to induce people to take up all these ritualistic processes, both the scripture and Caitanya Mahāprabhu recommend, "Chant the Hare Kṛṣṇa *mahā-mantra.*" This is the special advantage of this age—that by constant chanting of the Hare Kṛṣṇa *mahā-mantra*, one automatically becomes purified.

In His *Śikṣāṣṭaka*, Lord Caitanya describes the progressive benefits of chanting Hare Kṛṣṇa. First, *ceto-darpaṇa-mārjanam*. The beginning is cleansing the heart, because we are impure on account of dirty things within our heart, accumulated lifetime after lifetime in the animalistic way of life. So everything—advancement of spiritual life, culture, *tapasya*—is meant to cleanse the heart. And in this process of chanting the *mahā-mantra*, the first installment of benefit is the cleansing of the heart. *Ceto-darpaṇa-mārjanam*.

And when the heart is cleansed, then a person becomes eligible for being freed from the clutches of *māyā*, or the materialistic way of life. He understands that he is not this body—that he's a spirit soul, and that his business is therefore different from merely material concerns. He thinks, "Now I am engaged only in seeking these bodily comforts of life. These are not at all essential, because my body will change. Today, since I am in an American body, I think I have so many duties as an American man. Tomorrow I may be in an American dog body, and immediately my duty would change. So I can understand that these bodily concerns are not my real business. My real business is how to elevate myself—as a spirit soul—to the spiritual world, back to home, back to Godhead."

In this way the person who chants Hare Kṛṣṇa purifies his consciousness. Then his materialistic activity is stopped. He knows, "This is simply a waste of time. I must act spiritually." That is knowledge, which comes from cleansing the heart. The illusion of wrongly working on the basis of the bodily concept of life is overcome simply by the chanting of the Hare Kṛṣṇa *mahā-mantra*. This is the first installment of benefit from chanting.

And then there is *bhava-mahā-dāvāgni-nirvāpaṇam*: the process of stopping the blazing fire of material existence. Next, *śreyaḥ-kairava-candrikā-vitaraṇam*: his life becomes completely auspicious; and *vidyā-vadhū-jīvanam*: he becomes filled with transcendental knowledge. The next benefit is *ānandāmbudhi-vardhanam*: the ocean of transcendental bliss increases; and *pūrṇāmṛtāsvādanam*: he tastes the nectar of Kṛṣṇa consciousness at every step of life. In other words, his life becomes totally blissful. Finally, *sarvātma-snapanaṁ paraṁ vijāyate śrī-kṛṣṇa-saṅkīrtanam*: all glories to this *saṅkīrtana* movement, the chanting of the Hare Kṛṣṇa *mahā-mantra*!

So this *saṅkīrtana* movement is Caitanya Mahāprabhu's gift, and by taking up this chanting one attains *kevala-bhakti*, unalloyed devotion to the Lord. All the benefits of practicing austerities, penances, mystic yoga, and so on will be totally achieved simply by the chanting of the Hare Kṛṣṇa *mantra*. This is stated in the *Śrīmad-Bhāgavatam* [6.1.15]:

kecit kevalayā bhaktyā
vāsudeva-parāyaṇāḥ

agham̐ dhunvanti kārtsnyena
nīhāram iva bhāskaraḥ

Just as when the sun rises the all-pervading fog immediately disappears, so in this Kali-yuga, by the process of *bhakti-yoga*—especially by chanting the Hare Kṛṣṇa *mahā-mantra*—all one's sins are eradicated and one becomes fully reformed. In other words, one comes to the spiritual platform, and that is success in life.

THE PROCESS OF PURIFICATION

Puṣṭa Kṛṣṇa: Śrīla Prabhupāda, the next question somewhat echoes the previous one: "There are various *saṁskāras*, or purificatory ceremonies, prescribed for every civilized person, from birth to death. Many of these *saṁskāras* are not being observed today. Should they be revived?"

Śrīla Prabhupāda: The real aim of *saṁskāras* is to bring a rascal to the platform of knowledge. *Janmanā jāyate śūdraḥ*: by birth, everyone is the same—*śūdra*. In other words, one is without any knowledge. So the purpose of *saṁskāras* is to gradually bring a person who has no knowledge of spiritual life to the spiritual platform. As it is said, *saṁskārād bhaved dvijaḥ*: by the purificatory processes, one attains spiritual rebirth. That is essential.

Human life is the opportunity for understanding what one is and what the aim of one's life is. The aim of life is to go back home, back to Godhead. After all, we are part and parcel of God. Somehow or other, we are now in this material existence. So the real aim of life is to return to the spiritual world, where there is no struggle for existence—blissful, happy life. We want unending blissful life, but it is not possible in the material world That happiness is in the spiritual world. So our aim should be to go there, and every human being should be given the chance. That is real education. That is called *saṁskāra*, the process of purification.

Now, altogether there are *daśa-vidha-saṁskāra*, ten kinds of purificatory processes. So, in this age it is very difficult to follow them. but if one chants the Hare Kṛṣṇa *mahā-mantra* without any offense, under the guidance of a spiritual master, all these *saṁskāras* automatically become fulfilled, and one returns to his original, spiritual position.

Ahaṁ brahmāsmi—"I am a spirit soul." So, we are Brahman, spirit, and Kṛṣṇa is Param Brahman, the Supreme Spirit. As Arjuna said, *paraṁ brahma paraṁ dhāma pavitraṁ paramaṁ bhavān:* "You are the Supreme Spirit, the ultimate abode, the purest, the Absolute Truth." Kṛṣṇa is Brahman, or spirit, and I am also Brahman, but He's the Supreme Brahman, while I am minute Brahman. So my business is to serve Kṛṣṇa. That is the teaching of Lord Caitanya: *jīvera 'svarūpa' haya kṛṣṇera 'nitya-dāsa'*—"The real identity of the living being is that he is the eternal servant of Kṛṣṇa." So if one engages himself in his original, spiritual business, acting as the servant of Kṛṣṇa, then all processes of purification and reformation are fulfilled.

And that advantage of re-engagement in our original, spiritual business is given freely in this age: *kīrtanād eva kṛṣṇasya mukta-saṅgaḥ paraṁ vrajet*—"Simply by chanting the Lord's holy name, one achieves spiritual liberation." The reformatory processes, or *saṁskāras*, are meant for purifying a person so that he becomes *mukta-saṅgaḥ*, liberated from all the bad association of material existence and eligible to go back home, back to Godhead. So this is the special advantage of chanting the Hare Kṛṣṇa *mahā-mantra*.

The question was, "Should purificatory processes be revived?" They should be revived as far as necessary, but all of them cannot be revived in this age. So people should take to the chanting of the Hare Kṛṣṇa *mahā-mantra*. Then all reformation will be there, and people will come to the spiritual platform—*brahma-bhūtaḥ*, the realization of Brahman. Then *prasannātmā:* they'll be happy. *Na śocati na kāṅkṣati:* there will be no lamentation or needless hankering. *Samaḥ sarveṣu bhūteṣu:* they will see everyone on the spiritual platform. And finally, *mad-bhaktiṁ labhate param*. In this way they will come to the platform of devotional service, and then their life becomes successful. Is that question answered or not?

Puṣṭa Kṛṣṇa: Yes. Just one question I have, Śrīla Prabhupāda. You said that the *saṁskāras* should be revived as far as necessary?

Śrīla Prabhupāda: The essentials. For instance, to make one a *brāhmaṇa*, these four things are essential: no illicit sex, no meat-eating, no intoxication, no gambling. These essentials must be there; you cannot dispense with them. You must at least avoid sinful activities. Then one can practice Kṛṣṇa consciousness. As Kṛṣṇa says in the *Bhagavad-gītā* [7.28]:

yeṣāṁ tv anta-gataṁ pāpaṁ
janānāṁ puṇya-karmaṇām

te dvandva-moha-nirmuktā
bhajante māṁ dṛḍha-vratāḥ

"Persons who have acted piously in previous lives and in this life and whose sinful actions are completely eradicated are freed from the dualities of delusion, and they engage themselves in My service with determination."

You cannot become a devotee unless you give up sinful activity. Therefore you have to begin by following these four prohibitions. You have to avoid sinful activities like illicit sex, meat-eating, gambling, and intoxication, including tobacco, coffee, and tea. Then you'll gradually become completely sinless. On one side you have to follow restrictions, and on the other side you have to engage yourself in devotional service. To engage oneself in devotional service under the order of the spiritual master and the *śāstra* is the way to remain on the transcendental platform.

The transcendental platform means there is no sinful activity. It is above any question of "sinful." "Pious" and "sinful" activities are there only as long as you are on the material platform. "Good" and "bad," "pious" and "sinful"—these are all considerations on the material platform. But when you are on the transcendental platform, you are automatically without sin. Kṛṣṇa confirms this in *Bhagavad-gītā* [14.26]:

māṁ ca yo' vyabhicāreṇa
bhakti-yogena sevate
sa guṇān samatītyaitān
brahma-bhūyāya kalpate

The life of vice and the life of piety are within this material world, but when one is spiritually engaged, he is above the material plane, on the spiritual plane.

So the whole thing is that if you chant the Hare Kṛṣṇa *mahā-mantra* and give up these sinful activities, automatically you become reformed. You come to the spiritual platform. And in this way your life will become successful.

"FEEL THE ONENESS" . . . WITH A DIFFERENCE

Puṣṭa Kṛṣṇa: This next question is rather interesting, Śrīla Prabhupāda. "Is it not possible for all kinds of spiritualists—be they Advaitans [advocates of oneness of the self with God], Dvaitans [advocates of total difference between the self and God], or Viśiṣṭādvaitans [advocates of qualified oneness of the self with God]—come together instead of remaining isolated as warring factions?"

Śrīla Prabhupāda: Yes. This is the process taught by Caitanya Mahāprabhu—to bring all the Dvaitans and Advaitans together on one platform. Everyone has to understand that he is essentially a servant of God. The Advaitan wrongly thinks that he is absolutely one with God, that he himself is God. That is wrong. How can you become God? God is *ṣaḍ-aiśvarya-pūrṇam*, full in six opulences. He has all power, all wealth, all beauty, all fame, all knowledge, and all renunciation. So this *advaitan* idea is artificial—to think you're able to become God.

The *Dvaitans* stress that one is utterly different from God, that God is separate from the living entity. But actually, from the *Bhagavad-gītā* we understand that the living entities are part and parcel of God. And in the *Vedas* it is said, *nityo nityānāṁ cetanaś cetanānām:* both God and His creatures are living entities, though God is the chief. *Eko yo bahūnāṁ vidadhāti kāmān:* the difference between the two is that God maintains all the other living entities. That is a fact. We are maintained, and God is the maintainer. We are predominated—we are not independent—and God is the predominator. But because the predominated living entities are part and parcel of God, in quality they are one with God.

So Śrī Caitanya Mahāprabhu's philosophy is *acintya-bhedābheda:* the living entities are simultaneously one with and different from the Lord. The living entity is one in the sense that he is part and parcel of God. So if God were gold, the living entity would also be gold. That is oneness in quality. But God is great, and we are minute. In that way we are different. That is why Caitanya Mahāprabhu enunciated this philosophy of *acintya-bhedābheda:* inconceivable, simultaneous oneness with and difference from God. That is real philosophy.

So on the platform of this philosophy, everyone can come together, if they are reasonable. If they remain unreasonably stuck up in their own concocted philosophy, then it is difficult. But it is a fact that the living entity is eternally one with and different from God. Find this verse: *mamaivāṁśo jīva-loke.*

Hari-śauri:

mamaivāṁśo jīva-loke
jīva-bhūtaḥ sanātanaḥ

manaḥ ṣaṣṭhānīndriyāṇi
prakṛti-sthāni karṣati

"The living entities in this conditioned world are My eternal fragmental parts. Due to conditioned life, they are struggling very hard with the six senses, which include the mind." [Bg. 15.7]

Śrīla Prabhupāda: So if the living entity is eternally a fragmental part, how can he become one with the whole? The part is never equal to the whole. That is an axiomatic truth. So it is a wrong conception to try to become equal to God. The Māyāvādīs are trying to become God, but that is impossible. Let them try to become *godly*. *Godly* means "servant of God." That will make them perfect. The Vaiṣṇava philosophy teaches that we can remain in our natural position but act as a servant of God. That is perfect. But if the servant tries to become the master, that is artificial.

Of course, in the spiritual world there often seems to be no difference between the master and the servant. For instance, Kṛṣṇa's friends the cowherd boys—they do not know that Kṛṣṇa is God. They play with Him on equal terms. When Kṛṣṇa is defeated in play, He has to take His friend on His shoulder and carry him. The friends do not know who is God and who is not God. So that is the advanced spiritual conception. Of course, the difference is always there between God and the part-and-parcel living entities, but by the influence of God's internal potency, the understanding is covered. We can attain that position after many, many lives of pious activities. That is stated in the *Śrīmad-Bhāgavatam* [10.12.11]:

ittham satāṁ brahma-sukhānubhūtyā
dāsyaṁ gatānāṁ para-daivatena
māyāśritānāṁ nara-dārakeṇa
sākaṁ vijahruḥ kṛta-puṇya-puñjāḥ

The cowherd boys are playing with Kṛṣṇa. And who is Kṛṣṇa? He is the essence of *brahma-sukha*, spiritual bliss. He is Param Brahman, the Supreme Spirit. So the boys are playing with Param Brahman, though to an ordinary man He appears to be an ordinary child. How have the cowherd boys gotten the position of being able to play with Kṛṣṇa? *Kṛta-puṇya-puñjāḥ:* After many, many lives of pious activities, they have gotten the position of playing with Kṛṣṇa on equal terms.

So this is the conception of pure devotional service—that when you go to Goloka Vṛndāvana, Kṛṣṇa's abode, you love Kṛṣṇa so much that you will not distinguish between the Supreme Lord and His subordinates. The inhabitants of Kṛṣṇa's abode have such unflinching love for Kṛṣṇa. That is Vṛndāvana life. The cows, the calves, the trees, the flowers, the water, the elderly men, Kṛṣṇa's parents Nanda Mahārāja and Yaśodāmayī—everyone is intensely attached to Kṛṣṇa. Everyone's central point is Kṛṣṇa. Everyone is loving Kṛṣṇa so much that they do not know He is the Supreme Personality of Godhead.

Sometimes the residents of Vṛndāvana see Kṛṣṇa's wonderful activities and think, "Kṛṣṇa must be some demigod who has come here." They never recognize that Kṛṣṇa is the Supreme Personality of Godhead—or if they do, Kṛṣṇa makes them immediately forget. When

Kṛṣṇa manifested His pastimes on earth some five thousands years ago, He passed through many dangerous situations—so many demons were coming—and mother Yaśodā would chant *mantras* to protect Kṛṣṇa, thinking, "He may not be put into some calamity." Kṛṣṇa's family and friends never understood that Kṛṣṇa is God. Their natural love for Kṛṣṇa was so intense. Therefore Vṛndāvana life is so exalted. As Caitanya Mahāprabhu taught, *ārādhyo bhagavān vrajeṣa-tanayas tad-dhāma vṛndāvanam:* First of all, Kṛṣṇa—Vrajendra-nandana, the son of Nanda Mahārāja—is *ārādhya,* worshipable. Then, *tad-dhāma vṛndāvanam:* His *dhāma,* or abode—Vṛndāvana—is equally worshipable.

So these facts pertain to a higher standard of understanding. Only a devotee can understand that to become one with God is not a sublime idea. In Vṛndāvana the devotees want to become the father or mother of God—to control God with love. This fact the Māyāvādīs, or Advaitavādīs, cannot understand. Only pure devotees can understand these things. What is the benefit of becoming one with God?

Even other Vaiṣṇava philosophies cannot explain the higher relationships with God, which Caitanya Mahāprabhu explained. These are *vatsalya-rasa* [parenthood], and *madhurya-rasa* [conjugal love]. Caitanya Mahāprabhu especially taught that our relationship with Kṛṣṇa can be in conjugal love, *madhurya-rasa.*

But as for our general understanding, Lord Caitanya introduced the philosophy of *acintya-bhedābheda*—simultaneously one with and different from the Lord. That is explained by Kṛṣṇa in *Bhagavad-gītā* [15.7]:

mamaivāṁśo . . . jīva-bhūtaḥ—the living entities are part and parcel of God. So we are one with God, since we have God's qualities in minute degree. But God is the master, and we are always subordinate. *Eko bahūnāṁ yo vidadhāti kāmān:* we are protected, we are maintained, we are predominated. That is our position. We cannot attain the position of predominator. That is not possible.

HOW TO LOVE GOD

Puṣṭa Kṛṣṇa: Next question, Śrīla Prabhupāda. "As the world is coming to be divided into just two classes—atheist and theist—is it not advisable for all religions to come together? And what positive steps can be taken in this direction?"

Śrīla Prabhupāda: The steps to be taken have already been explained—this Kṛṣṇa consciousness movement. The atheist class and the theist class will always exist. This is the nature of the material world. Even at home—the father may be an atheist like Hiraṇyakaśipu, and the son a theist like Prahlāda. So atheists and theists will always exist—in the family, in the community, in the nation.

But the theists should follow the instructions of the *Bhagavad-gītā* and take shelter at Kṛṣṇa's lotus feet, giving up other, so-called religious principles. That will bring religious unity. Religion without a clear conception of God is humbug, bogus. Religion means to accept the order of God. So if you have no clear conception of God, if you do not know who God is, there is no question of accepting His order. Find this verse in the Sixth

Canto of *Śrīmad-Bhāgavatam: dharmaṁ tu sākṣād bhagavat-praṇītam*.

Hari-śauri:

dharmaṁ tu sākṣād-bhagavat praṇītam
na vai vidur ṛṣayo nāpi devāḥ
na siddha-mukhyā asurā manuṣyāḥ
kuto nu vidyādhara-cāraṇādayaḥ

"Real religious principles are enacted by . . ."

Śrīla Prabhupāda: Ah. "Real." Go on.

Hari-śauri: "Real religious principles are enacted by the Supreme Personality of Godhead. Although fully situated in the mode of goodness, even the great sages who occupy the topmost planets cannot ascertain the real religious principles, nor can the demigods or the leaders of Siddhaloka, to say nothing of the demons, ordinary human beings, Vidyadhāras, and Cāraṇas." [*Bhāg*. 6.3.19]

Śrīla Prabhupāda: Hm. Read the next verses also.

Hari-śauri:

svayambhūr nāradaḥ śaṁbhuḥ
kumāraḥ kapilo manuḥ
prahlādo janako bhīṣmo
balir vaiyāsakir vayam

dvādaśaite vijānīmo
dharmaṁ bhāgavataṁ bhaṭāḥ
guhyaṁ viśuddhaṁ durbodhaṁ
yaj jñātvāmṛtam aśnute

"Lord Brahma, Bhagavān Nārada, Lord Śiva, the four Kumāras, Lord Kapila [the son of Devahūti], Svāyambhuva Manu, Prahlāda Mahārāja, Janaka Mahārāja, Bhīṣmadeva, Bali Mahārāja, Śukadeva Gosvāmī, and I myself [Yamarāja] know the real religious principle. My dear servants, this transcendental religious principle, which is known as *bhāgavata-dharma*, or surrender unto the Supreme Lord and love for Him, is uncontaminated by the material modes of nature. This transcendental religious principle is very confidential and difficult for ordinary human beings to understand, but if by chance one fortunately understands it, he is immediately liberated, and thus he returns home, back to Godhead."

Śrīla Prabhupāda: So these *mahājanas*—Brahma, Nārada, Lord Śiva, and so on—they know what the principles of religion are. Religion means *bhāgavata-dharma*, understanding God and our relationship with God. That is religion. You may call it "Hindu religion" or "Muslim religion" or "Christian religion," but in any case, real religion is that which teaches how to love God. *Sa vai puṁsāṁ paro dharmo yato bhaktir adhokṣaje*: if by following some religious system you come to the platform of loving God, then your religious system is perfect. Otherwise, it is simply a waste of time—bogus religion, without a clear conception of God. So we have to understand what God is and what He says, and we have to abide by His orders. Then there is real religion, there is real understanding of God, and everything is complete.

Puṣṭa Kṛṣṇa: Śrīla Prabhupāda, one may ask why someone like Christ or Moses is not mentioned among the *mahājanas*.

Śrīla Prabhupāda: There are *mahājanas* among the Christian saints. They include Christ, and in addition to Christ, so many others—St. Matthew, St. Thomas, and so forth. These *mahājanas* are mentioned in the Bible. A *mahājana* is one who strictly follows the original religion and knows things as they are. And that means he must be coming in the *paramparā*, the system of disciplic succession.

For instance, Arjuna learned *Bhagavad-gītā* directly from Kṛṣṇa. Therefore Arjuna is a *mahājana*. So you should learn from Arjuna. You follow the way Arjuna acted and the way Arjuna understood Kṛṣṇa. Then *mahājano yena gataḥ sa panthāḥ*: you are following the *mahājana*—you are on the real path. Just as we are.

In these verses from *Śrīmad-Bhāgavatam* is a list of *mahājanas*, including Svāyambhu, or Lord Brahmā. So this *sampradāya* of ours is called the Brahma-sampradāya. Our *sampradāya* also includes Nārada, another *mahājana*. Śambhu, or Lord Śiva, is still another *mahājana*. He has his own *sampradāya*, the Rudra-sampradāya. And similarly, Lakṣmī, the goddess of fortune, has the Śrī-sampradāya.

So we must belong to one these *sampradāyas*. *Sampradāya-vihīnā ye mantrās te niṣphalā matāḥ*: if you do not belong to a bona fide *sampradāya*, originating from a *mahājana*, then your religious process is useless. You cannot concoct some religious system. So whether you follow the Christian *mahājanas* or the Vedic *mahājanas*, it doesn't matter. But you have to follow the *mahājanas*. If a Christian says, "I don't believe in St. Thomas," what kind of Christian is he? It doesn't matter which *mahājana* we are discussing. The real *mahājana* is he who is strictly following the principles enunciated by God. Then he is following a real religious system. Otherwise, there is no question of religion. The so-called follower is simply a *mano-dharmī*, a mental speculator. Mental speculation is not religion. Religion is the order of God, and one who follows that order—he is religious. That's all.

Puṣṭa Kṛṣṇa: Then as far as I can understand, Śrīla Prabhupāda, you're saying that there's no need to maintain sectarian labels, that there's one religion in the world.

Śrīla Prabhupāda: One religion exists already: how to love God. This is the one religion. Will the Christians say, "No, we don't want to love God"? Will the Muhammadans say, "No, no, we don't want to love God"? So religion means how to love God, and any religion which teaches how to love God—that is perfect. It doesn't matter whether you are Christian or Muslim or Hindu.

Dharmaṁ tu sākṣād bhagavat-praṇītam: "Real religion is directly enunciated by Bhagavān, the Supreme Personality of Godhead." So, Bhagavān, Lord Kṛṣṇa, says, "surrender unto Me." Of course, you cannot surrender until you love. For instance, you are surrendered to me. Even though I am not from your country, because you have love for me, you surrender. If I say, "do this," you'll do it. Why? Because you love me. So when will there be surrender to God? When one loves God—when one reaches the platform where he thinks, "O Lord, I love You; I can sacrifice everything for You." That is the basic principle of religion.

Therefore, that religion is perfect which teaches its followers how to love God. So let everyone come to this platform of loving God. That is Kṛṣṇa consciousness. We are teaching nothing but how to love God, how to sacrifice everything for God. That is real religion. Otherwise, it is all a bogus waste of time, simply a following of ritualistic ceremonies. That is not religion. That is superfluous. As stated in the *Śrīmad-Bhāgavatam* [1.2.8],

> *dharmaḥ svanuṣṭhitaḥ puṁsāṁ*
> *viṣvaksena-kathāsu yaḥ*
> *notpādayed yadi ratiṁ*
> *śrama eva hi kevalam*

"You are very good; you are following your religious principles very strictly. That's all right—but what about your love of God?" "Oh, that I do not know." So, the *Bhāgavatam* says, *śrama eva hi kevalam:* "Your religion is simply a waste of time—simply laboring. That's all. If you have not learned how to love God, then what is the meaning of your religion?"

But when you're actually on the platform of love of God, you understand your relationship with God: "I am part and parcel of God—and this dog is also part and parcel of God. And so is every other living entity." Then you'll extend your love to the animals also. If you actually love God, then your love for insects is also there, because you understand, "This insect has got a different kind of body, but he is also part and parcel of God—he is my brother." *Samaḥ sarveṣu bhūteṣu:* you look upon all living beings equally. Then you cannot maintain slaughterhouses. If you maintain slaughterhouses and disobey the order of Christ in the Bible—"Thou shall not kill"—and you proclaim yourself a Christian, your so-called religion is simply a waste of time. *Śrama eva hi kevalam:* your going to the church and everything is simply a waste of time, because you have no love for God. That foolishness is going on all over the world. People are stamping themselves with some sectarian label, but there is no real religion.

So if all people are to come together on one platform, they have to accept the principles of *Bhagavad-gītā*. The first principle is that Kṛṣṇa is the Supreme Personality of Godhead. If you do not accept in the beginning that Kṛṣṇa is the Supreme Lord, then try to understand this gradually. That is education. You can begin by accepting that there is *somebody* who is supreme.

Now, if I say, "Kṛṣṇa is the Supreme Lord," you may say, "Why is Kṛṣṇa the Supreme Lord? Kṛṣṇa is Indian." No. He is God. For example, the sun rises first over India, then over Europe. But that does not mean the European sun is different from the Indian sun. Similarly, although Kṛṣṇa appeared in India, now He has come to the Western countries through this Kṛṣṇa consciousness movement.

So you should try to understand whether Kṛṣṇa is God or not. But He is God. There is no doubt about it. If you have the intelligence to understand what God is, then try to understand. But Kṛṣṇa is God, undoubtedly. So take to Kṛṣṇa consciousness and abide by the order of Kṛṣṇa. Then everyone can come together on the same religious platform. One religion, Kṛṣṇa consciousness.

Puṣṭa Kṛṣṇa: Śrīla Prabhupāda, sometimes in our preaching activities we meet people who claim to be very devout Christians or Muslims but at the same time blaspheme Kṛṣṇa. Is it possible that such persons can actually be associates of God?

Śrīla Prabhupāda: No. If one is serious about understanding what God is, then he will accept Kṛṣṇa as the Supreme Lord. Once he knows what God is, he'll understand, "Here is God—Kṛṣṇa." If he remains in darkness and does not learn what God is, then how will he understand Kṛṣṇa? He'll understand Kṛṣṇa as one of us. That's all. But if he knows what God is, then he'll understand about Kṛṣṇa: "Yes, here is God."

For instance, if a person knows what gold is, then anywhere he comes upon gold, he'll understand, "Here is gold." He won't think gold is available in one shop only. And if a person knows what God is, what the meaning of "God" is, then in Kṛṣṇa he will find God in fullness. *Kṛṣṇas tu bhagavān svayam:* "Kṛṣṇa Himself is the Supreme Personality of Godhead." The *śāstra* explains what Bhagavān, or God, is, and how Kṛṣṇa is Bhagavān. You should understand and see from the activities of Kṛṣṇa whether He is or is not Bhagavān. It requires a good brain to understand. If I say, "Here is God," now it is up to you to test my statement. If you know what God is, then test my statement about Kṛṣṇa, and then you'll accept Him as God. If you do not know how to test my statement, then you may refuse to accept it. That is another thing. You may also accept iron as gold. That is your ignorance: you do not know what gold is. But if you actually know what God is, you will accept Kṛṣṇa as God. There is no doubt about it.

So this is the common platform—*Bhagavad-gītā*. Everyone, come and take to Kṛṣṇa consciousness.

Understand God and learn how to love Him, and your life will be perfect.

Puṣṭa Kṛṣṇa: But many people claim to have the best religion, Śrīla Prabhupāda.

Śrīla Prabhupāda: But we have to look at the result. How will we decide what is real religion? *Sa vai puṁsāṁ paro dharmaḥ yato bhaktir adhokṣaje:* by seeing whether the followers have learned how to love God. If one has no love of God, then what is the use of claiming that one's religion is the best? Where is the sign of love of Godhead? That is to be seen. Everyone will say, "My understanding is the best." But there must be practical proof.

If someone claims to have the best religion, we ask, "Tell us how to love God. What is your process of loving God? If you do not know your relationship with God and others' relationship with God, then how can you love God?" That process of loving God is lacking. Nobody can give a clear conception of God. If you have no understanding of what God is, where is the question of love? Love is not mere fantasy or imagination. You cannot love air. You love a person, a beautiful person. If you merely say, "I love the air, I love the sky," what question is there of love? There must be a person. So who is that person we want to love?

Unfortunately, most people have no personal conception of God. Nor can they describe the Lord's personal beauty, knowledge, strength—His fullness in the six personal opulences. There is no such description. They have some conception of God, but actually they do not know what God is. But religion means you must know God and love Him. Love is something tangible. It is not merely fantasy or imagination. So we Kṛṣṇa conscious people accept Kṛṣṇa as God, and we are worshiping Kṛṣṇa, and we are making progress.

Puṣṭa Kṛṣṇa: Recently a priest visited us and admitted that he didn't know what God looks like. He couldn't say anything about God, but he said he loved God.

Śrīla Prabhupāda: Then? What kind of love is it?

Puṣṭa Kṛṣṇa: Nor did he say his people were very enthusiastic about coming to church. He said, "At best they come once a week." He said that's all that is necessary.

Śrīla Prabhupāda: Well, love does not mean that you come once a week to my house. Love means you come to my house every day, give me some present, and take something from me. Śrīla Rūpa Gosvāmī describes the symptoms of love in his *Upadesamrta* [4]:

dadāti pratigṛhṇāti
guhyam ākhyāti pṛcchati
bhuṅkte bhojayate caiva
ṣaḍ-vidhaṁ prīti-lakṣaṇam

If you love somebody, you must give him something, and you must accept something from him. You must disclose your mind to him, and he should disclose his mind to you. And you should give him some eatable, and whatever eatable thing he offers, you accept. These six kinds of exchange develop love.

But if you do not even know the person, then where is the question of love? Suppose you love some boy or some girl, then you will give some present, and he or she gives you some present—that develops love. You give something to eat, and whatever he or she gives you to eat, you eat. You disclose your mind: "My dear such-and-such, I love you. This is my ambition." And he or she makes some disclosure. These are the exchanges of love.

But if there is no person-to-person meeting, where is the question of love? If I claim to love somebody, but I visit his house only once a week and ask, "Please give me such-and-such," where is the exchange of love? Love means there is some exchange. If you love somebody but you have not given anything to that person or taken anything from him, where is the love?

The conclusion is, religion means to love God, and that means you must know who God is. There is no alternative. You must know the person who is God. Then you can have loving exchanges with Him. That we are teaching. We are asking our disciples to rise early in the morning and offer *maṅgala ārati*, then *bhoga ārati*, to the Lord in His form as the Deity in the temple. Are we such fools and rascals that we are wasting time worshiping a "doll"? Sometimes people think like that. But that is not a fact. When you enter the temple, you know definitely, "Here is Kṛṣṇa. He is God, and we must love Him like this." That is the superexcellence of this Kṛṣṇa consciousness movement. We do everything definitely, on the positive platform. Is that clear? Does anyone have any further question?

Pradyumna: Śrīla Prabhupāda, you're saying we must know God before we can love Him. So that means devotional service is preceded by knowledge.

Śrīla Prabhupāda: Yes, that is the process given in the

Bhagavad-gītā. There are eighteen chapters, and the whole eighteen chapters are education—how to know God. When Arjuna at last comes to complete awareness, he accepts, "Kṛṣṇa, You are *param brahma*, the Supreme Personality of Godhead." Then Arjuna surrendered, as Kṛṣṇa advised—*sarva-dharmān parityajya*. But unless you know God, how will you surrender? If some third-class man comes and says, "Surrender to me," will you do that? "Why should I surrender to you?" You must know, "Now, here is God. I must surrender." Eighteen chapters describe God and how to know God, and then Kṛṣṇa proposes, "Surrender unto Me." Then Arjuna does it: "Yes." So without knowing God, how can you surrender to Him? It is not possible.

So the *Bhagavad-gītā* is the science of how to know God. The preliminary science. If you want to know more, then read *Śrīmad-Bhāgavatam*. And if you are in intense love with God, read *Caitanya-caritāmṛta*—how your love for God can be still more intensified. That is *Caitanya-caritāmṛta*. So *Bhagavad-gītā* is the preliminary book: to understand God and surrender. And from the surrendering point, further progress—that is S*rimad-Bhāgavatam*. And when the love is intense, to make it more intensified—that is *Caitanya-caritāmṛta*. Caitanya Mahāprabhu was mad after God. He cried, *śūnyāyitaṁ jagat sarvaṁ govinda viraheṇa me*: "I find everything vacant without Kṛṣṇa." That is the supreme ecstasy.

So these things cannot happen without love. If you love somebody and he's not there, you find everything vacant. So Śrī Caitanya Mahāprabhu felt this way about Kṛṣṇa—lover and beloved. *Śūnyāyitaṁ jagat sarvaṁ govinda viraheṇa me*: "I see everything vacant without Govinda." That is the supreme stage of love. Is that clear or not?

Pradyumna: There's just one more thing, Śrīla Prabhupāda. What's the minimum knowledge one must have to . . .

Śrīla Prabhupāda: God is great. That's all. God is great. Kṛṣṇa proved that He's great. Therefore He's God. Everyone says, "God is great." *Allah-u- akbar*, the Muslims say: "God is great." And Hindus say, *param brahma*: "You are the Supreme Spirit." So God is great. And when Kṛṣṇa was present, He proved that He is all-great. Therefore He's God. If you accept that God is great, and if you find somebody who is great in everything, then He is God. How can you deny it? You can see how great Kṛṣṇa is simply by considering His *Bhagavad-gītā*. Five thousand years have passed since Kṛṣṇa spoke *Bhagavad-gītā*, and still it is accepted as the greatest book of knowledge all over the world. Even people from other religions who are really learned accept it. That is proof of the greatness of Kṛṣṇa—this knowledge. Who can give such knowledge? That is the proof that He is God. Kṛṣṇa has all opulences in full, including knowledge. Other than here in Kṛṣṇa's words, where is such knowledge throughout the whole world? Every line is sublime knowledge. If you study *Bhagavad-gita* scrutinizingly, you'll understand that Kṛṣṇa is the Supreme Lord.

THE WAY TO PEACE

Puṣṭa Kṛṣṇa: Next question, Śrīla Prabhupāda. "Do you envision a different role for the Vedic culture in the Western countries, where the influence of other great religions has been felt for centuries?"

Śrīla Prabhupāda: No. There is no "different role." God is one. God cannot be two. As Kṛṣṇa states in the *Bhagavad-gītā* [7.7], *mattaḥ parataraṁ nānyat kiñcid asti dhanañjaya:* "There is no authority superior to Me." That is God. Now people have to understand that Kṛṣṇa is God. There is no "different role" for the Vedic culture. The role is the same worldwide. Five thousand years ago, Kṛṣṇa said, "I am the supreme authority. There is no authority superior to Me." He is still so. Therefore we are simply attempting to introduce Kṛṣṇa.

Previously nobody attempted to introduce the supreme authority, Kṛṣṇa, all over the world. We are just trying to introduce Kṛṣṇa, following the orders of Śrī Caitanya Mahāprabhu, who appeared five hundred years ago. He is Kṛṣṇa, and He wanted this Kṛṣṇa consciousness to be spread all over the world:

pṛthivīte āche yata nagarādi-grāma
sarvatra pracāra haibe mora nāma

"In every town and village throughout the world," said Lord Caitanya, "the chanting of My holy name will be heard." Kṛṣṇa is not just for India. He is for everyone, because He is God. In *Bhagavad-gītā* He affirms, *ahaṁ bīja-pradaḥ pitā:* "I am the seed-giving father of all living entities"—not just the living entities in the human society, but also all other living entities, like the aquatics, the insects, the plants, the birds, and the beasts.

Everything is there in the Vedic culture, but this culture of Kṛṣṇa consciousness, which is summarized in *Bhagavad-gītā As It Is*, had not been preached properly. Everyone had interpreted *Bhagavad-gītā* in his own way, to satisfy his own whims. We are just trying for the first time to present *Bhagavad-gītā* as it is, and it is becoming effective. So this is not a "different role" for the Vedic culture. It is the actual role. Nobody had tried for it; therefore Kṛṣṇa had been unknown in the Western countries. But even though we have been attempting to introduce Him for only a few years, still, because it is reality, Kṛṣṇa consciousness is being accepted. So it is not a new role for the Vedic culture. The role is already there—to preach Kṛṣṇa consciousness.

That is Caitanya Mahāprabhu's vision. He says especially to people born in India:

bhārata-bhūmite manuṣya-janma haila yāra
janma sārthaka kari' kara para-upakāra

"Anyone who has taken his birth as a human being in India, Bhāratavarṣa, should make his life successful and work for the upliftment of the whole world." Indians are meant for this business—for the upliftment of the whole world—because all over the world people are unaware of Kṛṣṇa. So anyone who is born in India should attempt to broadcast the message of *Bhagavad-gītā* and Kṛṣṇa. That is the order of Caitanya Mahāprabhu.

This is not a new role for the Vedic culture. The role is already there. Five hundred years ago, Caitanya Mahāprabhu spoke of it. But all the various swamis and *yogis* who came here—they never introduced Kṛṣṇa as the Supreme Personality of Godhead. Now it is being done, and people are accepting, naturally. This is the Kṛṣṇa consciousness movement.

So if everyone joins—either Indian or non-Indian—in this movement, there will be one religion and there will be peace. Peace will prevail. This is the only way.

bhoktāraṁ yajña-tapasāṁ
sarva-loka-maheśvaram
suhṛdaṁ sarva-bhūtānāṁ
jñātvā māṁ śāntim ṛcchati

"A person in full consciousness of Me, knowing Me to be the ultimate beneficiary of all sacrifices and austerities, the Supreme Lord of all planets and demigods, and the benefactor and well-wisher of all living entities, attains peace from the pangs of material miseries." This is the way to attain *śānti*, peace. Understand Kṛṣṇa—that He is the supreme enjoyer, the supreme proprietor, and the supreme friend of everyone. "Accept Kṛṣṇa as your friend. You'll be happy." This is the message of Kṛṣṇa consciousness.

RETURN TO REAL LIFE

Puṣṭa Kṛṣṇa: Śrīla Prabhupāda, the final question is: "What is your view regarding proselytizing or preaching?"

Śrīla Prabhupāda: We are simply attempting to bring people to the real understanding. Kṛṣṇa says, *mamaivamso jīva-bhūtaḥ:* all living entities are part and parcel of Me. He says, *sarva-yoniṣu kaunteya . . . ahaṁ bīja-pradaḥ:* "Of all forms of life, I am the seed-giving father." In other words, the natural position is that every living entity—animals, plants, and human beings, including Indians, Americans, Czechs—everyone is part and parcel of Kṛṣṇa.

So our Kṛṣṇa consciousness movement is not a process of trying to convince people of some speculative idea. This movement is actually bringing people to their real position—that they're all part and parcel of Kṛṣṇa. It is not artificial proselytizing: "You are Christian; now become a Hindu." It is not like that. This movement is actually bringing people back to their natural position—part and parcel of God.

The effects of artificial proselytizing will not stand. But when one comes to the real understanding of his position, then that will continue. This Kṛṣṇa consciousness movement is that real understanding—bringing everyone back to his original position. At the present moment everyone is in a diseased condition: people are thinking they are something other than servants of Kṛṣṇa. Now this movement is trying to bring everyone to the position of recognizing that they are eternal servants of Kṛṣṇa.

This movement is not some kind of rubber-stamp proselytizing—"You were Christian; now you are Hindu." After all, if one does not know what his position is, what benefit will he derive by simply being stamped "Hindu"?

Puṣṭa Kṛṣṇa: No benefit. He'll still be in ignorance of his real, spiritual identity.

Śrīla Prabhupāda: If you keep someone on the ignorant platform, then what is the benefit of making a Christian or a Muslim into a Hindu? No, artificially changing someone into a Hindu will not help. One must know the philosophy of life. One must know what God is. One must learn how to love God. That is real life.

END

Worship at Home

Chanting the Hare Kṛṣṇa Mantra

The first principle in devotional service is to chant the Hare Kṛṣṇa *mahā-mantra* (*mahā* means "great"; *mantra* means "sound that liberates the mind from ignorance"):

Hare Kṛṣṇa, Hare Kṛṣṇa, Kṛṣṇa Kṛṣṇa, Hare Hare
Hare Rāma, Hare Rāma, Rāma Rāma, Hare Hare

You can chant these holy names of the Lord anywhere and at any time, but it is best to set a specific time of the day to regularly chant. Early morning hours are ideal.

As you chant, pronounce the names clearly and distinctly, addressing Kṛṣṇa in a prayerful mood. When your mind wanders, bring it back to the sound of the Lord's names. Chanting is a prayer to Kṛṣṇa that means "O energy of the Lord [Hare], O all-attractive Lord [Kṛṣṇa], O Supreme Enjoyer [Rāma], please engage me in Your service." The more attentively and sincerely you chant these names of God, the more spiritual progress you will make.

God has kindly made it very easy for us to chant His names, and He has also invested all His powers in them. Therefore the names of God and God Himself are identical. This means that when we chant the holy names we are directly associating with God and being purified. Therefore we should always try to chant with devotion and reverence.

When you chant alone, it is best to chant on *japa* beads (available from Temple Services, at one of the addresses given in the advertisement at the end of this book). This helps you fix your attention on the holy name. Each strand of *japa* beads contains 108 small beads and one large bead, the head bead. Begin on a bead next to the head bead and gently roll it between the thumb and middle finger of your right hand as you chant the full Hare Kṛṣṇa *mantra*. Then move to the next bead and repeat the process. In this way, chant on each of the 108 beads until you reach the head bead again. This is one round of *japa*. Then, without chanting on the head bead, reverse the beads and start your second round on the last bead you chanted on.

Aside from chanting *japa*, you can also sing the Lord's holy names in *kīrtana*. While you can perform *kīrtana* individually, it is generally performed with others. A melodious *kīrtana* with family or friends is sure to enliven everyone. ISKCON devotees use traditional melodies and instruments, especially in the temple, but you can chant to any melody and use any musical instruments to accompany your chanting. As Lord Caitanya said, "There are no hard and fast rules for chanting Hare Kṛṣṇa." One thing you might want to do, however, is order some *kīrtana* and *japa* audiotapes from Temple Services.

Setting Up Your Altar

You will likely find that your *japa* and *kīrtana* are especially effective when done before an altar. Lord Kṛṣṇa and His pure devotees are so kind that they allow us to worship them even through their pictures. It is something like mailing a letter: You cannot mail a letter by placing it in just any box; you must use the mailbox authorized by the government. Similarly, we cannot imagine a picture of God and worship that, but we can worship the authorized picture of God, and Kṛṣṇa accepts our worship through that picture.

Setting up an altar at home means receiving the Lord and His pure devotees as your most honored guests. An ideal place would be clean, well lit, and free from drafts and household disturbances, such as a wall shelf, a mantelpiece, a corner table, or the top shelf of a bookcase will do. Don't make your altar inaccessible. Put it where is will be in plain view.

What do you need for an altar? Here are the essentials:

1. A picture of Śrīla Prabhupāda.
2. A picture of Lord Caitanya and His associates.
3. A picture of Śrī Śrī Rādhā-Kṛṣṇa.

If you're interested in more elaborate Deity worship, ask any of the ISKCON devotees or write to Temple Services.

The first person we worship on the altar is the spiritual master. The spiritual master is not God. Only God is God. But because the spiritual master is His dearmost servant, God has empowered him, and therefore he deserves the same respect as that given to God. He links the disciple with God and teaches him the process of *bhakti-yoga*. He is God's ambassador to the material world. When a president sends an ambassador to a foreign country, the ambassador receives the same respect as that accorded the president, and the ambassador's words are as authoritative as the president's. Similarly, we should respect the spiritual master as we would God, and revere his words as we would His.

There are two main kinds of *gurus:* the instructing *guru* and the initiating *guru*. Everyone who takes up the process of *bhakti-yoga* as a result of coming in contact with ISKCON owes an immense debt of gratitude to Śrīla Prabhupāda. Before Śrīla Prabhupāda left India in 1965 to spread Kṛṣṇa consciousness abroad, almost no one outside India knew anything about the practice of pure devotional service to Lord Kṛṣṇa. Therefore, everyone who has learned of the process through his books, his *Back to Godhead* magazine, his tapes, or contact with his followers should offer respect to Śrīla Prabhupāda. As the founder and spiritual guide of the International Society for Krishna Consciousness, he is the instructing *guru* of us all.

As you progress in *bhakti-yoga*, you may eventually want to accept initiation. At present there are many spiritual masters in ISKCON. To learn how you can get in touch with them for spiritual guidance and association, ask a devotee at your nearby temple, or write to the president of one of the ISKCON centers listed at the end of this book.

The second picture on your altar should be one of Lord Caitanya and His four leading associates. Lord Caitanya is the incarnation of God for this age. He is Kṛṣṇa Himself, descended in the form of His own devotee to teach us how to surrender to Him, specifically by chanting His holy names and performing other activities of *bhakti-yoga*.

And of course your altar should have a picture of the Supreme Personality of Godhead, Lord Śrī Kṛṣṇa, with His eternal consort, Śrīmatī Rādhārāṇī. Śrīmatī Rādhārāṇī is Kṛṣṇa's spiritual potency. She is devotional service personified, and devotees always take shelter of Her to learn how to serve Kṛṣṇa.

You can arrange the pictures in a triangle, with the picture of Śrīla Prabhupāda on the left, the picture of Lord Caitanya and His associates on the right, and the picture of Rādhā and Kṛṣṇa, which, if possible, should be slightly larger than the others, on a small raised platform behind and in the center. Or you can hang the picture of Rādhā and Kṛṣṇa on the wall above.

Prasādam: How to Eat Spiritually

If we place an iron rod in a fire, before long the rod becomes red hot and acts just like fire. In the same way, food prepared for and offered to Kṛṣṇa with love and devotion becomes completely spiritualized. Such food is called Kṛṣṇa *prasādam*, which means "the mercy of Lord Kṛṣṇa."

Eating only food offered to Kṛṣṇa is the perfection of vegetarianism. In itself, being a vegetarian is not enough; after all, even pigeons and monkeys are vegetarians. But when we go beyond vegetarianism to a diet of *prasādam*, our eating becomes helpful in achieving the goal of human life—reawakening the soul's original relationship with God. In the *Bhagavad-gītā* Lord Kṛṣṇa says that unless one eats only food that has been offered to Him in sacrifice, one will suffer the reactions of *karma*.

How to Prepare and Offer Prasādam

First of all, you need to know what is offerable and what is not. In the *Bhagavad-gītā*, Lord Kṛṣṇa states, "If one offers Me with love and devotion a leaf, a flower, a fruit, or water, I will accept it." From this verse it is understood that we can offer Kṛṣṇa foods prepared from milk products, vegetables, fruits, nuts, and grains. (Write to Temple Services for one of the many Hare Kṛṣṇa cookbooks.) Meat, fish, and eggs are not offerable. And a few vegetarian items are also forbidden—garlic and onions, for example, which are in the mode of darkness. (*Hing*, or asafetida, is a tasty substitute for them in cooking and is available at most Indian groceries or from Temple Services.) Nor can you offer to Kṛṣṇa coffee or tea that contain caffeine. If you like these beverages, purchase caffeine-free coffee and herbal teas.

Be aware that you may find meat, fish, and egg products mixed with other foods; so be sure to read labels carefully. For instance, some brands of yogurt and sour cream contain gelatin, a substance made from the horns, hooves, and bones of slaughtered animals. Also, make sure the cheese you buy contains no rennet, an enzyme extracted from the stomach tissues of slaughtered calves.

In preparing food, cleanliness is the most important principle; so keep your kitchen very clean. Always wash your hands thoroughly before entering the kitchen. While preparing food, do not taste it, for you are cooking the meal not for yourself but for the pleasure of Kṛṣṇa. Arrange portions of the food on dinnerware kept especially for this purpose; no one but the Lord should eat from these dishes. The easiest way to offer food is simply to pray, "My dear Lord Kṛṣṇa, please accept this food," and to chant each of the following prayers three times while ringing a bell:

1. Prayer to Śrīla Prabhupāda:

nama oṁ viṣṇu-pādāya kṛṣṇa-preṣṭhāya bhū-tale
śrīmate bhaktivedānta-svāmin iti nāmine

namas te sārasvate deve gaura-vāṇī-pracāriṇe
nirviśeṣa-śūnyavādi-pāścātya-deśa-tāriṇe

"I offer my respectful obeisances unto His Divine Grace A. C. Bhaktivedanta Swami Prabhupāda, who is very dear to Lord Kṛṣṇa, having taken shelter at His lotus feet. Our respectful obeisances are unto you, O spiritual master, servant of Bhaktisiddhānta Sarasvatī Gosvāmī. You are kindly preaching the message of Lord Caitanyadeva and delivering the Western countries, which are filled with impersonalism and voidism."

2. Prayer to Lord Caitanya:

namo mahā-vadānyāya kṛṣṇa-prema-pradāya te
kṛṣṇāya kṛṣṇa-caitanya-nāmne gaura-tviṣe namaḥ

"O most munificent incarnation! You are Kṛṣṇa Himself appearing as Śrī Kṛṣṇa Caitanya Mahāprabhu. You have assumed the golden color of Śrīmatī Rādhārāṇī, and You are widely distributing pure love of Kṛṣṇa. We offer our respectful obeisances unto You."

3. Prayer to Lord Kṛṣṇa:

namo brahmaṇya-devāya go-brāhmaṇa-hitāya ca
jagad-dhitāya kṛṣṇāya govindāya namo namaḥ

"I offer my respectful obeisances unto Lord Kṛṣṇa, who is the worshipable Deity for all *brāhmaṇas*, the well-wisher of the cows and the *brāhmaṇas*, and the benefactor of the whole world. I offer my repeated obeisances to the Personality of Godhead, known as Kṛṣṇa and Govinda."

Remember that the real purpose of preparing and offering food to the Lord is to show your devotion and gratitude to Him. Kṛṣṇa cares more about the devotion of your offering than the offering itself.

After offering the food to the Lord, wait at least five minutes for Him to partake of the preparations. Then you should transfer the food from the special dinnerware and wash the dishes and utensils you used for the offering. Now you and any guests may eat the *prasādam*. While you eat, try to appreciate the spiritual value of the food. Remember that because Kṛṣṇa has accepted it, it is nondifferent from Him, and therefore by eating it you will become purified.

ISKCON CENTERS AROUND THE WORLD

ISKCON is a world wide community of devotees of Krishna dedicated to the principles of bhakti-yoga. Classes are held in the evenings during the week, and a special feast and festival is held every Sunday afternoon. Write, call, or visit for further information.

NORTH AMERICA

CANADA

Montreal, Quebec—1626 Pie IX Boulevard, H1V 2C5/ Tel. (514) 521-1301 **Ottawa, Ontario**—212 Somerset St. E., K1N 6V4/ Tel. (613) 233-1884 **Regina, Saskatchewan**—1279 Retallack St., S4T 2H8/ Tel. (306) 525-1640 **Toronto, Ontario**—243 Avenue Rd., M5R 2J6/ Tel. (416) 922-5415 **Vancouver, B.C.**—5462 S.E. Marine Dr., Burnaby V5J 3G8/ Tel. (604) 433-9728

FARM COMMUNITY

Ashcroft, B.C.—Saranagati Dhama, Box 99, Ashcroft, B.C. V0K 1A0

RESTAURANTS

Toronto—Hare Krishna Dining Room (at ISKCON Toronto) **Vancouver**—Hare Krishna Buffet (at ISKCON Vancouver)

U.S.A.

Arcata, California—P.O. Box 4233, Arcata, CA / Tel. (707) 826-9219 **Atlanta, Georgia**—1287 Ponce de Leon Ave. N.E., 30306/ Tel. (404) 377- 8680 **Baltimore, Maryland**—200 Bloomsbury Ave., Catonsville 21228/ Tel. (301) 744-9537 **Boise, Idaho**—1615 Martha St., 83706/ Tel. (208) 344-427 **Boston, Massachusetts**—72 Commonwealth Ave., 02116/ Tel. (617) 247-8611 **Chicago, Illinois**—1716 W. Lunt Ave., 60626/ Tel. (312) 973-0900 **Cleveland, Ohio**—11206 Clifton Blvd., 44102/ Tel. (216) 651-6670 **Dallas, Texas**—5430 Gurley Ave., 75223/ Tel. (214) 827-6330 **Denver, Colorado**—1400 Cherry St., 80220/ Tel. (303) 333-5461 **Detroit, Michigan**—383 Lenox Ave., 48215/ Tel. (313) 824-6000 **Gurabo, Puerto Rico**—ISKCON, HC 1, Box 8440, 00658-9763/ Tel. (809) 737-5222
Gainesville, Florida—214 N.W. 14th St., 32603/ Tel. (904) 336-4183 **Honolulu, Hawaii**—51 Coelho Way, 96817/ Tel. (808) 595-3947 **Houston, Texas**—1320 W. 34th St., 77018/ Tel. (713) 686-4482 **Laguna Beach, California**—285 Legion St., 92651/ Tel. (714) 494-7029 **Lansing, Michigan**—1914 E. Michigan Ave., 48912/ Tel. (517) 484-2209 **Long Island, New York**—197 S. Ocean Ave., Freeport, 11520/ Tel. (516) 378-6184 **Los Angeles, California**—3764 Watseka Ave., 90034/ Tel. (213) 836-2676 **Miami, Florida**—3220 Virginia St., 33133/Tel. (305) 442-7218 **New Orleans, Louisiana**—2936 Esplanade Ave., 70119/ Tel. (504) 486-8605 **New York, New York**—305 Schermerhorn St., Brooklyn 11217/ Tel.(718) 855-6714 **Philadelphia, Pennsylvania**—51 W. Allens Lane, 19119/ Tel. (215) 247-4600 **Philadelphia, Pennsylvania**—529 South St., 19147/ Tel. (215) 829-0399 **St. Louis, Missouri**—3926 Lindell Blvd., 63108/ Tel. (314) 535-8085 **San Diego, California**—1030 Grand Ave., Pacific Beach 92109/ Tel. (619) 483-2500 **San Francisco, California**—84 Carl St., 94117/ Tel. (415) 753-8647 **San Francisco, California**—2334 Stuart St., Berkeley 94705/ Tel. (415) 644-1113 **Seattle, Washington**—1420 228th Ave. S.E., Issaquah 98027/ Tel. (206) 391-3293 **Tallahassee, Florida**—1323 Nylic St. (mail: P.O. Box 20224, 32304)/ Tel. (904) 681-9258 **Topanga, California**—20395 Callon Dr., 90290/ Tel. (213) 455-1658 **Towaco, New Jersey**—(mail: P.O. Box 109, 07082)/Tel. (201) 299-0970 **Walla Walla, Washington**—314 E. Poplar, 99362/ Tel. (509) 529-9556 **Washington, D.C.**—10310 Oaklyn Dr., Potomac, Maryland 20854/ Tel. (301) 299-2100

FARM COMMUNITIES

Carriere, Mississippi (New Talavan)—Route 2, Box 449, 39426/ Tel. (601) 798-8533 **Gainesville, Florida (New Ramana-reti)**—Box 819, Alachua 32615/ Tel. (904) 462-9046 **Gurabo, Puerto Rico (New Govardhana Hill)**—(contact ISKCON Gurabo) **Hillsborough, North Carolina (New Goloka)**—Rt. 6, Box 701, 27278/ Tel. (919) 732-6492 **Mulberry, Tennessee (Murari-sevaka)**—Murari Project, Rt. No. 1, Box 146-A, 37359/ Tel. (615) 759-7331 **Port Royal, Pennsylvania (Gita-nagari)**—R.D. No. 1, Box 839, 17082/ Tel. (717) 527-4101

RESTAURANTS

Chicago—Govinda's Buffet (at ISKCON Chicago) **Boulder, Colorado**—917 Pleasant St., 80302 / Tel. (303) 444-7005 **Dallas**—Kalachandji's (at ISKCON Dallas) **Denver**—(at ISKCON Denver) **Detroit**—Govinda's (at ISKCON Detroit) / Tel. (313) 331-6740 **Laguna Beach**—Gauranga's (at ISKCON Laguna Beach) **Lansing, Michigan**—Govinda's Diners' Club (at ISKCON Lansing) **Los Angeles**—Govinda's, 9624 Venice Blvd., Culver City 90230/ Tel. (213) 836-1269 **Philadelphia**—Govinda's, 529 South St., 19147 / Tel. (215) 829-0077 **Provo, Utah**—Govinda's Buffet, 260 North University, 84601 /Tel. (801) 375-0404 **Santa Cruz, California**—Gauranga's, 503 Water St., 95060 / Tel. (408) 427-0294

EUROPE

GREAT BRITAIN AND NORTHERN IRELAND

Belfast, Northern Ireland—140 Upper Dunmurray Lane, Belfast/ Tel. (0232) 681328 **Birmingham, West Midlands**—84 Stanmore Rd., Edgebaston **Dublin, Eire**—Hare Krishna Centre, 3 Temple Lane, Dublin 2/ Tel. 353-1-6795887 **Leicester, England**—21 Thoresby St., North Evington, Leicester/ Tel. (0533)-762587 **Liverpool, England**—135 Northumberland St., Liverpool, L8 8AY/ Tel. (051)-709 9188 **Manchester, England**—20 Mayfield Road, Whalley Range, Manchester M16 8FT/ Tel. (061)-226 4416 **Newcastle upon Tyne, England**—21 Leazes Park Rd./Tel. (091)- 222-0150 **London, England (city)**—10 Soho St., London W1V 5FA / Tel. (71) 437-3662 **London, England (country)**—Bhaktivedanta Manor, Letchmore Heath, Watford, Hertfordshire WD2 8EP/ Tel. (092385) 7244 **Scotland**—Karuna Bhavan, Bankhouse Road, Lesmahagow, Lanarkshire/ Tel. (0555)-894790

FARM COMMUNITIES

Hare Krishna Island, N. Ireland—Derrylin, County Fermanagh, BT92 9GN, N. Ireland/ Tel. (3657) 21512 **London, England**—(contact Bhaktivedanta Manor)

RESTAURANTS

London, England—Govinda's, 9–10 Soho St. / Tel. (71) 437-3662

ITALY

Bologna—Via Nazionale 124, 40065-Pianoro (BO)/ Tel. (51) 774-034 **Bergamo**—Villaggio Hare Krishna, Via Galileo Galilei, 41, 24040 Chignolo D'isola (BG)/ Tel. 035-490706 **Catania**—Via San Nicolo al Borgo 28, 95128 Catania, Sicily/ Tel. (95) 522-252 **Naples**—Via Vesuvio, N33, Ercolano LNA7/ Tel. (81) 739-0398 **Padua**—Via delle Granze 107, 35040

Loc. Camin (PD)/ Tel. (49) 760-007 **Rome**—Via di Tor Tre Teste 142, 00169 Roma/ Tel. (06) 262913

FARM COMMUNITY

Florence (Villa Vrindavan)—Via Communale degli Scopeti 108, S. Andrea in Percussina, San Cascian Val di Pesa (FI) 5002/Tel. (55) 820-054

RESTAURANTS

Milan—Govinda's, Via Valpetrosa 3/5, 20123 Milano / Tel. (2) 862-417 **Rome**—Govinda's, Via di San Simone 73/A, 00186 Roma/ Tel. (6) 654-1973

OTHER COUNTRIES

Amsterdam, Holland—Krishna Dham, 225 Ruysdaelkade, 1072 AW/ Tel.(020) 751 404 **Antwerp, Belgium**—184 Amerikalei 2000/ Tel. (03) 237-0037, 237-0038 **Athens, Greece**—Poseidonos 27, Ilioupoli, 16 345/ Tel. 01-993-7080 **Barcelona, Spain**—c/de L'Oblit, 67-08026/ (93) 347-9933 **Belgrade, Yugoslavia**—Vaisnavska vjerska zajednica, Sumatovacka 118, 11000 Beograd/ Tel. (0) 11/ 434-183 **Bellinzona, Switzerland**—New Nandagram, al Chiossascio, 6594 ContoneTI/Tel. 092-622747 **Berlin, W. Germany**—Bhakti Yoga Zentrum, Friedrichstrasse 31, 1000Berlin 61/ Tel. (030) 2514372 **Brussels, Belgium**—49 rue Marche aux Poulets,1000 Bruxelles/ Tel. (02)513 86 05/04 **Budapest, Hungary**—M.K.T.H.K., J. Kalmar, Marton U. 52, 1038 Budapest **Copenhagen, Denmark**—Kongens Tvaerej 11, DK-2000 Frederiksberg/ Tel. (01) 86-85-81 **Durbuy, Belgium**—Chateau de Petit Somme, Durbuy 5482/ Tel. 086-322926 **Gothenburg, Sweden**—Grimmeredsvaegen 103, 421 69 Vaestra Froelunda/Tel. 031-290966 **Grodinge, Sweden**—Korsnas Gard, 14792 Grodinge/Tel. 0753-29151 **Hamburg, W. Germany**—Holzbrucke 2a, 2000 Hamburg/ Tel. (040) 8503464 **Heidelberg, W. Germany**—Kurfuerstenalage 5, D-6900/ Tel. 06221 15101 **Helsinki, Finland**—Eljaksentie 9, 00370 Helsinki **Hoerup, W. Germany**—Neuhoerup 1, D-2391 Hoerup **Lisbon, Portugal**—Rua Fernao Lopes, 6, Cascais 2750 (mail: Apartado 2489, Lisboa 1112)/Tel. (11) 286 713 **Malmoe, Sweden**—Center for Vedisk Kultur, Remegentsgata 14, S-211 42 Malmoe/ Tel. (040) 127181 **Moscow, USSR**—Contact ISKCON Office of Soviet Affairs, Almviks Gard, 15300 Jarna, Sweden/ Tel. (46) 0755-52050 **Munich, W. Germany**—Brodstrasse 12, D-8000 Muenchen 82 **Oslo, Norway**—Senter for Krishnabevissthet, Skolestien 11, 0373 Oslo 3 **Paris, France**—31 Rue Jean Vacquier, 93160 Noisy le Grand/ Tel. 45921018; 43043263 **Prague, Czechoslovakia**—Hare Krishna, Na Nrazi 5, 18000 Praha 8 / Tel. 42-2-821438 **Pregrada, Yugoslavia**—Davor Bateli, Gorika 5/6, Pregrada / Tel. 38-49-73176 **Stockholm, Sweden**—Fridhemsgatan 22, 112 40 Stockholm/ Tel. 08-549002 **Turku, Finland**—ISKCON, Sairashuokeenkatu 8A1, 20140 Turku 14/Tel. (9) 21 308981 **Vienna, Austria**—Center for Vedic Studies, Rosenackerstrasse 26, 1170 Vienna/ Tel. (0222) 455830 **Warsaw, Poland**—Towarzystwo Swiadomosci Kryszny—Bhakti Yoga W PRL, 02-770 Warasawa130, skr. pocztowa 257 **Zurich, Switzerland**—Bergstrasse 54, 8030 Zuerich/ Tel. (01) 262-33-88 **Zurich, Switzerland**—Preyergrasse 16, CH-8001 Zuerich

FARM COMMUNITIES

Jandelsbrunn, W. Germany (Nava-Jiyada-Nrsimha-Ksetra)—Zielberg 20, D-8391/ Tel. 85831332 **Brihuega, Spain (New Vraja Mandala)**—(Santa Clara) Brihuega, Guadalajara/ Tel. (11)280018 **Denmark**—Gl. Kirikevej 3, 6650 Broerup/ Tel. 45-75-392921 **Jarna, Sweden**—Almviks Gard, 15300 Jarna/ Tel. (0755) 52050, (0755) 52073 **Roch d'Or, Switzerland**—The Gokula Project, Vacherie Dessous, Ch-2913 Roch d'Or/ Tel. 066-766160 **Valençay, France (New Mayapur)**—Luçay-Le-Male, 36 600/ Tel. (54) 40-23-53

RESTAURANTS

Malmoe, Sweden—Higher Taste, Amiralsgatan 6, S-211 55 Malmoe/ Tel. (040) 970600 **Zurich, Switzerland**—Govinda's Restaurant, Preyergasse 16, 8001 Zurich / Tel. (01) 251-8859

AUSTRALASIA

AUSTRALIA

Adelaide—74 Semaphore Rd., Semaphore, S. A. 5019/Tel. (8) 493 200 **Brisbane**—95 Bank Road, Graceville, Q.L.D. (mail: P.O. Box 83, Indooroopilly 4068)/ Tel. (07) 379-5455 **Melbourne**—197 Danks St., Albert Park, Victoria 3206 (mail: P.O. Box 125)/ Tel. (03) 699-5122 **North Sydney**—180 Falcon St., N. Sydney, N.S.W. 2060 (mail: P.O. Box 220, Cammeray, N.S.W. 2060)/ Tel. (02) 955-6164 **Perth**—Sri Sri Gaura Nitai Perth Mandir, 144 Railway Parade (cnr. The Strand), Bayswater (mail: P.O. Box 102, Bayswater, W. A. 6053)/ Tel. (09) 370 1552, Fax. (09) 272 6636 **Sydney**—112 Darlinghurst Rd., Darlinghurst, N.S.W. 2010 (mail: P.O. Box 159, Kings Cross,N.S.W. 2011)/ Tel. (02) 3575162

FARM COMMUNITIES

Bambra (New Nandagram)—Oak Hill, Dean's Marsh Road, Bambra, VIC 3241/ Tel. (052)88738 **Millfield, N.S.W.**—New Gokula Farm, Lewis Lane (off Mt.View Rd. Millfield near Cessnock), N. S. W. / Tel. 049-981852 **Murwillumbah (New Govardhana)**—Tyalgum Rd., Eungella, via Murwillumbah N. S. W. 2484 (mail: P.O. Box 687)/ Tel. (066) 721903

RESTAURANTS

Adelaide—Crossways, 79 Hindley St., Adelaide, S.A. 5000 / Tel. (08) 231-5258 **Brisbane**—Crossways, First Floor, 99 Elisabeth Street **Melbourne**—Crossways, First Floor, 123 Swanston St., Melbourne, Victoria 3000 / Tel. (03) 650 2939 **Melbourne**—Gopal's, 139 Swanston St., Melbourne, Victoria 3000 / Tel. (03) 650-1578 **North Sydney**—Gopal's, 180 Falcon St., N. Sydney, N.S.W. 2060 / Tel. (02) 926164 **Perth**—Hare Krishna Food for Life, 129 Barrack St., Perth, WA 6000 / Tel. (09) 325 2168 **Sydney**—Govinda's Upstairs and Govinda's Take-away (both at ISKCON Sydney) / Tel. (075) 501642

NEW ZEALAND AND FIJI

Auckland, New Zealand (New Varshan)—Hwy. 18, Riverhead (next to Huapai Golf Course)(mail: R.D. 2, Kumeu, Auckland)/ Tel. (9) 4128075 **Christchurch, New Zealand**—83 Bealey Ave. (mail: P.O. Box 25-190 Christchurch)/ Tel. (3) 61965 **Labasa, Fiji**—Delailabasa (mail: Box 133)/Tel. 82916 **Lautoka, Fiji**—5 Tavewa Ave. (mail: P.O. Box 125)/ Tel. 64112 **Rakiraki, Fiji**—Rewasa, Rakiraki (mail: P.O. Box 94243) **Suva, Fiji**—Nasinu 7 1/2 miles (P.O. Box 6376)/ Tel. 391-282 **Wellington, New Zealand**—6 Shotter St., Karori (mail: P.O. Box 2753, Wellington)/ Tel. (4) 764445

RESTAURANTS

Auckland, New Zealand—Gopal's, 1st Floor., Civic House, 291 Queen St. / Tel. 15 (9) 3034885 **Christchurch, New Zealand**—Gopal's, 143 Worcester St. / Tel. 67-035 **Lautoka, Fiji**—Gopal's, Corner of Yasawa St. & Naviti St. / Tel. 62990 **Suva, Fiji**—Gopal's, 18 Pratt St. / Tel. 62990 **Suva, Fiji**—Gopal's, 37 Cumming St. / Tel. 312259

AFRICA

Abeokuta, Nigeria—Ibadan Rd., Obantoko, behind NET

(mail: P.O. Box 5177) **Abidjan, Ivory Coast**—01 BP 8366, Abidjan

Accra, Ghana—582 Blk. 20, Odokor, Official Town (mail: P.O. Box 01568, Osu) **Buea, Cameroon**—Southwest Province (mail: c/o Yuh Laban Nkesah, P and T, VHS) **Cape Town, South Africa**—17 St. Andrews Rd., Rondebosch 7700/ Tel. (21) 689 1529 **Durban (Natal), S. Africa**—Chatsworth Circle, Chatsworth 4030 (mail: P.O. Box 56003)/ Tel. (31) 435-815 **Freetown, Sierra Leone**—13 Bright St., Brookfields (mail: P.O. Box 812, Freetown) **Johannesburg, South Africa**—14 Goldreid St., Hillbrow, Johannesburg 2001/Tel. (11) 666-2716 **Harare, Zimbabwe**—46 Crowhill Rd. (mail: P.O. Box 2090)/ Tel. 8877801 **Kitwe, Zambia**—3122 Gandhi Close, Buyantanshi (mail: P.O. Box 20242, Kitwe)/ Tel. 215-630 **Lagos, Nigeria**—No. 2 Murtala Mohammed International Airport Expressway, Mafaluku (mail: P.O. Box 8793, Lagos) **Phoenix, Mauritius**—Hare Krishna Land, Pont Fer, Phoenix (mail: P. O. Box 108, Quartre Bornes, Mauritius) / Tel. (230) 696-5804 **Mombasa, Kenya**—Hare Krishna House, Sauti Ya Kenya and Kisumu Rds. (mail P.O. Box 82224, Mombasa)/ Tel. 312248 **Nkawkaw, Ghana**—P.O. Box 69, Nkawkaw **Nairobi, Kenya**—Muhuroni Close, off West Nagara Rd. (mail: P.O. Box 28946, Nairobi)/ Tel. 744365

Port Harcourt, Nigeria—2 Eligbam Rd. (corner of Obana Obhan St.), G.R.A. II (mail: P.O. Box 4429, Trans Amadi) **Tokoradi, Ghana**—64 Windy Ridge (mail: P.O. Box 328) **Warri, Nigeria**—1 Ogunu St., Bendel Housing Estate, Ugborikoro (P.O. Box 1922, Warri)/ Tel. 053-230-262

FARM COMMUNITIES

Lusaka, Zambia—Plot 4/288 Chingololo Rd., Makeni (mail: P.O. Box 35658, Lusaka)/ Tel. 210-578

Mauritius (Vedic Farm)—ISKCON Vedic Farm, Hare Krishna Road, Beau Bois, Bon Accuel / Tel. 418-3955

RESTAURANT

Durban, S. Africa—Govinda's (contact ISKCON Durban)

ASIA

INDIA

Agartala, Tripura—Assam-Agartala Rd., Banamalipur, 799001 **Ahmedabad, Gujarat**—7, Kailas Society, Ashram Rd., 380 009/ Tel. 449935 **Bamanbore, Gujarat**—N.H. 88, Surendranagar Dist./ Tel. 97 **Bangalore, Karnataka**—Hare Krishna Hill, 1 'R' Block, Chord Road, Rajajinagar 560 010/ Tel. 359 856 **Baroda, Gujarat**—Hare Krishna Land, Gotri Rd., 390 015/ Tel. 326299 and 66499 **Bhayandar, Maharashtra**—Shivaji Chowk, Station Road, Bhayandar (West), Thane 401101/ Tel. 6982987 and 6982621 **Bhubaneswar, Orissa**—National Highway No. 5, Nayapali, 751 001/ Tel. 53125 **Bombay, Maharashtra**—Hare Krishna Land, Juhu 400 049/ Tel. 6206860 **Calcutta, W. Bengal**—3C Albert Rd., 700 017/ Tel. 443757, 434265, 446075 **Chandigarh, Punjab**—Hare Krishna Land, Dakshin Marg, Sector 36-B, 160 036/ Tel. 44634 **Coimbatore, Tamil Nadu**—Padmam 387, VGR Puram, Alagen Road-1, 641-001/Tel. 4597

Gauhati, Assam—Ulubari Charali, Gauhati 781 001/ Tel. 31208 **Guntur, A.P.**—Opp. Sivalayam, Peda Kakani 522 509 **Hardwar, U.P.**—Pahala Mala, Brittany Cottage, Kharkhari 249 401 (mail: P.O. Box 14) **Hyderabad, A.P.**—Hare Krishna Land, Nampally Station Rd., 500 001/ Tel. 551018, 552924 **Imphal, Manipur**—Hare Krishna Land, Airport Road, 795 001/ Tel. 21587 **Madras, Tamil Nadu**—59, Burkit Rd., T. Nagar, 600 017/ Tel. 443266 **Mayapur, W. Bengal**—Shree Mayapur Chandrodaya Mandir, P.O. Shree Mayapur Dham, Dist. Nadia/ Tel. 31 (Swarup Ganj) **Moirang, Manipur**—Nongban Ingkhon, Tidim Rd./ Tel. 795133 **Nagpur, Maharashtra**—70 Hill Road, Ramnagar, 440 010/ Tel. 33513 **New Delhi**—M-119 Greater Kailash 1, 110 048/ Tel. 6412058, 6419701 **New Delhi**—14/63, Punjabi Bagh, 110 026/ Tel. 5410782 **Pandharpur, Maharashtra**—Hare Krishna Ashram, across Chandrabhaga River, Dist. Sholapur, 413 304 **Patna, Bihar**—Rajendra Nagar Road No. 12, 800 016/ Tel. 50765 **Pune, Maharashtra**—4 Tarapoor Rd., Camp, 411 001/ Tel. 60124 and 64003 **Secunderabad, A.P.**—9-1-1 St. John's Road, 500 026/Tel. 825232 **Silchar, Assam**—Ambikapatti, Silchar, Cachar Dist., 788004 **Siliguri, W. Bengal**—Gitalpara 734 401/ Tel. 26619

Surat, Gujarat—Rander Rd., Jahangirpura, 395 005/ Tel. 84215 **Tirupati, A.P.**—K.T. Road, Vinayaka Nagar 517 507/ Tel. 2285 **Trivandrum, Kerala**—T.C. 224/1485, WC Hospital Rd., Thycaud, 695 014/ Tel. 68197 **Udhampur, Jammu and Kashmir**—Prabhupada Nagar, Udhampur 182 101/Tel. 496 P.P. **Vrindavana, U.P.**—Krishna-Balaram Mandir, Bhaktivedanta Swami Marg, Raman Reti, Mathura Dist. 281 124/ Tel. (5664) 82478

FARM COMMUNITIES

Ahmedabad, Gujarat—Nityananda Seva Ashram, Odhav Rd. (near Octroi Naka), Odhav 382 410 Tel. 886 382 **Ahmedabad District, Gujarat**—Hare Krishna Farm, Katwada (contact: ISKCON Ahmedabad) **Assam**—Karnamadhu, Dist. Karimganj

Chamorshi, Maharashtra—78 Krishnanagar Dham, District Gadhachiroli, 442 603 **Hyderabad, A.P.**—P.O. Dabilpur Village, Medchal Tq., R.R. District, 501 401/ Tel. 552924 **Mayapur, W. Bengal**—(contact ISKCON Mayapur)

RESTAURANTS

Bombay, Maharashtra—Govinda's (at Hare Krishna Land)
Vrindavana—Krishna-Balaram Mandir Guesthouse

OTHER COUNTRIES

Bali, Indonesia—(Contact ISKCON Jakarta) **Bangkok, Thailand**—P.O. Box 15, Prakanong, Bangkok **Cagayan de Oro, Philippines**—30 Dahlia St., Ilaya Carmen, 900 Cagayan de Oro (c/o Sepulveda's Compound) **Chittagong, Bangladesh**—Caitanya Cultural Society, Sri Pundarik Dham, Mekhala, Hathazari Tel. 10 (city office and mail: 23 Nandan Kanan, Chittagong)/ Tel. 202219 **Colombo, Sri Lanka**—188 New Chetty St., Colombo 13/ Tel. 33325 **Hong Kong**—27 Chatam Road South, 6/F, Kowloon/ Tel. 3 7396818 **Iloilo City, Philippines**—13-1-1 Tereos St., La Paz, Iloilo City Iloilo/ Tel. 73391 **Jakarta, Indonesia**—P.O. Box 2694, Jakarta 10001 **Kathmandu, Nepal**—Vishnu Gaun Panchayat Ward No. 2, Budhanilkantha/ Tel. 4-10368 **Kuala Lumpur, Malaysia**—Lot 9901, Jalan Awan Jawa, Taman Yari, off 5 1/2 Mile, Jalan Kelang Lama, Petaling/ Tel. 7830172 **Manila, Philippines**—170 R. Fernandez, San Juan, Metro Manila/ Tel. 707410 **Osafiya, Israel**—Hare Krishna, Osafiya 30900/ Tel. 4-391150 **Taipei, Taiwan**—(mail: c/o ISKCON Hong Kong) **Tehran, Iran**—Keshavarz-Dehkadeh Ave., Kamran St. No. 58/ Tel. 658870 **Tel Aviv, Israel**—57 Frishman St., POB 48163, Tel Aviv 61480/ Tel. (03) 246325 **Tokyo, Japan**—2-41-12 Izumi, Suginami-ku, Tokyo T168/ Tel. (3) 327-1541

FARM COMMUNITIES

Bogor, Indonesia—Govinda Kunja (contact ISKCON Jakarta) **Cebu, Philippines (Hare Krishna Paradise)**—231 Pagsabungan Rd., Basak, Mandaue City/ Tel. 83254 **Perak, Malaysia**—Jalan Sungai Manik, 36000 Teluk Intan, Perak

RESTAURANTS

Cebu, Philippines—Govinda's, 26 Sanchiangko St. **Hong Kong**—The Higher Taste Vegetarian Dining Club (at ISKCON

Hong Kong) **Kuala Lumpur, Malaysia**—Govinda's, 16-1 Jalan Bunus Enam Masjid, India/Tel. 03-2986785

LATIN AMERICA

BRAZIL

Belem, PA—Av. Gentil Bittencourt, 1002–Nazare, CEP 66040 **Belo Horizonte, MG**—Rua St. Antonio, 45, Venda Nova, CEP 31510 **Brazilia, DF**—Q. 706-Sul, Bloco C, Casa 29, HIGS, CEP 70350/ Tel. (061) 242-7579 **Curitiba, PR**—Rua Jornalista Caio Machado, 291, B. Sta. Quiteria, CEP 80320 **Florianopolis, SC**—Rua 14 de julho, 922, Estreito, CEP 88075 **Fortaleza, CE**—Rua Jose Laurenço, 2114, Aldeota, CEP 60115 **Goiania, GO**—Rua C-60, Quadra 123, Lt-11, Setor Sudoeste, CEP 74305 **Manaus, AM**—Avenida 7 de Setembro, 1599, Centro, CEP 69003/ Tel: (092) 232-0202 **Pitajul, SP**—Av. Brazil, 306, CEP 16600 **Porto Alegre, RS**—Rua Tomas Flores, 331, Bomfim, CEP 90210 **Recife, PE**—Rua Reverendo Samuel Falcao, 75, Madalena, CEP 50710 **Rio de Janeiro, RJ**—Rua Armando Coelho de Freitas, 108, Barra da Tijuca, CEP 22620 **Salvador, BA**—Rua Alvaro Adorno, 17, Brotas, CEP 40240/ Tel: (071) 244-1072

Santos, SP—Rua Nabuco de Araujo, 151, Embare, CEP 11025/ Tel. (0132) 38-4655 **Sao Paulo, SP**—Avenida Angelica, 2583, Consolaçao, CEP 01227/ Tel. (011) 59-7352

FARM COMMUNITIES

Caruaru, PE—Comunidade Nova Vrajadhama, Distrito de Murici (mail: CP. 283, CEP 55100) **Pindamonhangaba, SP (Nova Gokula)**—Comunidade Nova Gokula, Barrio do Ribeirao Grande (mail: Caixa Postal 067 Pindamonhangaba, SP, CEP 12400)

RESTAURANT

Belem, Para (Shri Krishna Prasada)—Av. Gentil Bittencourt, Passagem Mac Dowell, 96 (entre Dr. Moraise Benjamin Constant / Tel (091) 222-1886

MEXICO

Guadalajara—Pedro Moreno 1791, Sector Juarez, Jalisco/ Tel. 26-12-78 **Mexico City**—Gobernador Tiburcio Montiel No. 45, Col. San Miguel Chapultepec, C.P. 11850, Mexico D.F. **Monterrey**—Zaragoza 1007, nte. Zona centro/ Tel. 74-69-76 **Tijuana**— Mutualismo 516 Primero C **Vera Cruz**—Calle 3, Carebelas No. 784, Fraccionamienito Reforma/ Tel. 50759

FARM COMMUNITY

La Primavera, Jalisco —(contact ISKCON Guadalajara)

PERU

Arequipa—Jerusalen 402/ Tel. 229523 **Cuzco**—San Juan de Dios 285 **Lima**—Pasaje Solea 101 Santa Maria-Chosica/ Tel. 910891 **Lima**—Schell 634 Miraflores **Lima**—Av. Garcilazo de la Vega 1670-1680/Tel. 259523

FARM COMMUNITY

Hare Krishna-Correo De Bella Vista—DPTO De San Martin

RESTAURANTS

Arequipa—(at ISKCON Arequipa) **Cuzco**—Espaderos 128 **Lima**—Schell 634 Miraflores

OTHER COUNTRIES

Asuncion, Paraguay—Centro Bhaktivedanta, Alberdi 1603 esq. 4ta., Asuncion/ Tel. 595-21-70066 **Bahia Blanca, Argentina**—Centro de Estudios Vedicos, F. Sanches 233, (8000) Bahia Blanca **Bogota, Colombia**—Calle 63A, #10-62, Chapinero/ Tel. 249-5797 **Bogota, Colombia**—Transversal 1a, #56-22, Alto Chapinero/ Tel. 255-8742 **Buenos Aires, Argentina**—Centro Bhaktivedanta, Andonaegui 2054, (1431)/Tel. 5155 **Cali, Colombia**—Avenida 2 EN, #24N-39/ Tel. 68-88-53 **Caracas, Venezuela**—Avenida Berlin, Quinta Tia Lola, La California Norte/Tel: (58-2) 225463 **Christ Church, Barbados**—31 Goodland Park/ Tel. (809) 42-84209 **Cochabamba, Bolivia**—Av. Heroinas E-0435 Apt. 3 (mail: P. O. Box 2070, Cochabamba

Concepcion, Chile—Nonguen, 588/ Tel. 23150 **Cordoba, Argentina**—Montevideo 950, Paso de los Andes/ Tel. (051) 262229 **Crabwood Creek, Guyana**—Grant 1803, Sec. D, Corentyne, Berbice **Cuenca, Ecuador**—Entrada de Las Pencas 1– Avenida de Las Americas/ Tel: (593-7) 825211 **Essequibo Coast, Guyana**—New Navadvipa Dham, Mainstay, Essequibo Coast **Georgetown, Guyana**—24 Uitvlugt Front, West Coast Demerara **Guatemala, Guatemala**—Apartado Postal 1534 **Guayaquil, Ecuador**— 6 de Marzo 226 y V. M. Rendon/Tel. (593-4) 308412 y 309420 **La Paz, Bolivia**—P. O. Box 10278, Miraflores, La Paz **Montevideo, Uruguay**—Centro de Bhakti-Yoga, Pablo de Maria 1427, Montevideo/ Tel. 598-2484551 **Panama, Republic of Panama**—Via las Cumbres, entrada Villa Zaita, frente a INPSA No. 1(mail: P.O. Box 6-29-54, Panama)

Pereira, Colombia—Carrera 5a, #19-36 **Quito, Ecuador**—Inglaterra y Amazonas **Rosario, Argentina**—Centro de Bhakti-Yoga, Paraguay 556, (2000)Rosario/Tel. 54-41-252630 **San Jose, Costa Rica**—Centro Cultural Govinda, 235 mtrs. norte del Banco Anglo, San Pedro (mail: Apdo. 166,100)/ Tel. 34-1218

San Salvador, El Salvador—Avenida Universitaria 1132, Media Quadra al sur de la Embajada Americana, San Salvador (mail: P.O. Box 1506)/Tel. 25-96-17 **Santiago, Chile**—Carrera 330/ Tel. 698-8044 **Santo Domingo, Dominican Republic**—Calle Cayetano Rodriquez No. 254 **Trinidad and Tobago, West Indies**—Orion Drive, Debe/Tel. 647-739 **Trinidad and Tobago, West Indies**—Prabhupada Ave. Longdenville, Chaguanas

FARM COMMUNITIES

Argentina (Bhaktilata Puri)—Casilla de Correo No 77, 1727 Marcos Paz, Pcia. Bs.As., Republica Argentina **Bolivia**—Contact ISKCON Cochabamba **Colombia (Nueva Mathura)**—Cruzero del Guali, Municipio de Caloto, Valle del Cauca Tel. 612688 en Cali **Ecuador (Nueva Mayapur)**—Ayampe (near Guayaquil) **Guyana**—Seawell Village, Corentyne, East Berbice **Guyaquil, Ecuador**—(Contact ISKCON Guyaquil) **San Jose, Costa Rica**—Granja Nueva Goloka Vrindavana, Carretera a Paraiso, de la entrada del Jardin Lancaster (por Calle Concava), 200 metros as sur (mano derecha)Cartago (mail: Apdo. 166, 1002)/ Tel. 51-6752 **San Salvador, El Salvador**—Carretera a Santa Ana, Km. 34, Canton Los Indios, Zapotitan, Dpto. de La Libertad

RESTAURANTS

Cochabamba, Bolivia—Gopal Restaurant, calle Espana N-0250 (Galeria Olimpia), Cochabamba(mail: P. O. Box 2070, Cochabamba **Guatemala, Guatemala**—Callejor Santandes a una cuadra abajo de Guatel, Panajachel Solola **Quito, Ecuador**—(contact ISKCON Quito) **San Salvador, El Salvador**—25 Avenida Norte 1132 **Santa Cruz, Bolivia**—Snack Govinda, Av. Argomosa (1ero anillo).